Chapter 1

Poverty

Today, political groups routinely decry the horror of so few people holding most of the wealth. These groups imply that the extremely rich people have control over the world and make people poor. Political groups say that this difference should be offset by taking money from the rich and giving it to the poor. They believe that people are poor because they have not been treated fairly.

Today, people do not become poor because of someone becoming rich. Bill Gates of Microsoft fame became a billionaire and not one person became poor as a result. In fact, many people became rich and millions more are employed because of his success. Actually, what would help the poor is if we could somehow multiply the Bill Gates of the world. Think of all the jobs that would be created.

An overriding issue I think, is that the poor no longer have a mental picture of how their lives could be. Having a home with a yard for kids to play in, a nice car, friends, a good job, are not even in their dreams. After generations of being poor, their idea of a good life is more likely a steady supply of heroin. All the counseling and training in the world isn't going to change that. The only answer is to break the cycle.

The historical argument of whether to appease the poor by making them happy in their circumstance or try to reduce their numbers is an age-old question. In the last 50 years or so, the make them happy approach has dominated the scene. Today the poor have free health care, food stamps, housing, cell phones, cable TV, and free education. Many things only the middle classes acquire in other countries. Maybe that is good. American should be rated Number 1 for poor people.

> *"I am for doing good to the poor, but...I think the best way of doing good to the poor, is not making them easy in poverty but leading or driving them out of it."*
>
> **-Benjamin Franklin, 1766 (On the Price of Corn and Management of the Poor)**

Outside of making sure we are humane in our treatment of the poor, as a nation we have many choices for guiding the poor. We can make the poor person's life easier.   Because of the large numbers of poor, it actually makes sense to supply the poor cell phones and so on, so they can call for services they need.

However, is making life easy for the poor really humane? On the other hand, are we guarantying a permanent number of poor people? Are we just making the poor, hopelessly poor? Isn't it inhumane not to aggressively push, pull, and tug the poor from their failed patterns and prevent them from passing their plight on to the next generations? If there were only 10 poor people in the USA, wouldn't it still be our obligation to try to reduce the number?

Perhaps the single largest source of poor in America is the steady growth of single-parent households. Poverty patterns are like criminal and drug abuse patterns in that it is best to stop them before they start. Once they become habits, there really is no solution. The billions of dollars we pour into welfare and criminal justice do not alleviate the problem and appear to make the situation worse.

Today in many cases young teens have babies and start receiving aid for housing, food, and medical care. This allows moving to an apartment nearby where the teen mother and the usually much older "Pseudo Daddy" can hang out. This looks glamorous and encourages other teen girls to get pregnant quit school and go on welfare. Eventually most "Pseudo Daddies" disappear." The single mother with no education or job skill continues life in poverty likely having more children to avoid being cut from the welfare rolls. While her children grow and have babies to maintain the poverty cycle.

> *"Delaware becomes the first state to completely ban child marriage and others likely to follow suit"*

Daily Mail

By age 30, two-thirds of all women will have had a child out of wedlock. The average age of first birth for women who drop out of high school is 20, while their average married age is 25. Eighty-three percent of first births to non-high school graduates are to unwed mothers.

> *"A U.S. Census Bureau study found that the percentage of children living in single-parent households increased from 12*

percent in 1960 to 31 percent in 2016. During that same timeframe, "the percentage of children living with only their mother nearly tripled."

FOX NEWS

Almost 50 percent of all first births happening outside of wedlock.

"Young unmarried parents are statistically more likely to be poor, have emotional or behavioral problems and are less likely to do well in school,"

according to information released by the New York City Office of the Mayor in conjunction with a teen pregnancy PSA campaign. Young men are also less likely to be involved with their children.

National Marriage Project director Bradford Wilcox, an associate professor of sociology in University of Virginia's College of Arts & Sciences, said in a press release.

"What they often don't realize is that children born outside of marriage are significantly more likely to be exposed to a revolving cast of caretakers and the social, emotional and financial fallout associated with family instability and single parenthood."

A high percentage of children born to poor unwed mothers are the same underperforming schoolchildren with social adjustment problems that become the drug abusers and prisoners in our jails. As with reducing crime, we need to get involved early to prevent the poverty pattern from taking hold.

Single women's reasons for having a child include,

• To keep a usually much older male friend (statutory rape)

• To qualify for welfare

• To carry out motherly instincts

• To gain attention

• To relieve boredom

- To relieve depression

- To prove adulthood

- To get away from parents and home life

We have only one option to reduce poverty and end the cycle. **That is to, not let poor single mothers raise their children.**

Currently, the kids of most single mothers are raised in decrepit housing with questionable nutrition and healthcare, go to the worst schools, are raised by unrelated alcoholics and drug addicts, have no educational support, are more likely to be illiterate suffer abuse and have little access to safe healthy developmental activities.

Children raised in these conditions are more likely not to graduate from high school, suffer abuse use drugs and commit a crime. Statistically, the only exposure to an adult male many poor children may have will be to someone who uses illegal drugs and has committed multiple crimes. I hate to say it, but almost anything would be an improvement for most of these kids. Remember, 83% percent of first births to non-high school graduates are to unwed mothers. How else can we break the poverty cycle?

Recently there was a major hullabaloo because children were being separated from adults possibly parents who had entered the country illegally. Desperate political adversaries who made the fuss ignored the actual situation of these children. These children did not arrive at the border after a nice trip in the family SUV. Overnighting at a Comfort Inn and stopping at McDonald's for lunch along the way. More likely they spent hours in the back of a truck and slept on the ground. Eating a little bread and raw carrots along the way.

Once in detention, they had 3 square meals, air-conditioning, beds to sleep on, medical care and a play area. How traumatic could that separation have been?

Even though this has been tried 80 years ago, it should not deter us today. Poverty level single mothers should not be allowed to keep their children. Modern child residence care could provide excellent nutrition, healthcare, safe clean conditions, playgrounds and organized activities of all kinds. Residence care employees would have extensive background checks. The residences could have cameras throughout with live video piped into child services to oversee activity and care. School-age children could attend public schools. Cities would be encouraged with incentives to build facilities and support child residence care.

This concept would have a tremendously positive impact on young teens, as all of the irrational reasons for having a baby would be lost. The only choice for the mother after having a baby would be to go back to school. No more babies having babies, no welfare cash and no hangout apartment, fewer abortions. The number of babies born to young unwed mothers would drop dramatically, I assure you.

The reason people are poor in the United States is that they made bad choices. People will say this is an oversimplification. They will say, the poor have no parents, they were hooked on drugs, and their housing conditions were terrible. Can we really remove the blame from the individual and give them a free ride? How do we look others born into the same conditions in the eye, who did not choose to use drugs, did not choose to quit school, who did choose to go to work instead of collect welfare? My own father died when I was in 6th grade. I could have failed miserably and used his death as my excuse.

Poor people make poor choices. Should we continue to tell the poor as their numbers multiply on welfare or in prison, you made some bad choices? On the other hand, should we start early educating people about making good choices, then push and pull them until they take the positive opportunities they have?

Most states have a set of welfare packages for the poor. They include some cash, food, housing, medical and job training assistance. Cash assistance is usually limited to 4 or 5 years with extensions during slow economic periods. In addition, the federal government provides subsidized housing, food stamps, income tax rebates and free medical care. It is easy to see how someone can get addicted to this lifestyle.

Several states have adopted requirements to try to force those on welfare into activities that try to keep recipients in the job market such as, 20 hours a week of classes and so on. These steps are commendable however, it is an uphill battle as poverty habits have had generations to take hold and they are almost impossible to break.

In Southeast Michigan, it was clear that people learned to work the welfare system. Once a married man gained some seniority in an auto factory, it was a common practice to divorce his wife so she and the kids would qualify for welfare benefits. The husband would still live at home. One worker told me, "If they are dumb enough to give me the benefits, I'm gonna take um. We're getting an extra $450 a month."

A routine practice also was to have people on welfare sign up for federally subsidized job training programs that offered weekly cash stipends. After the training, it was clear the trainees did not intend to go to work.

We should require the poverty level healthy to leave their residence often. One reason is to create a pattern, which mimics work life. Another is it would control calorie intake. Obesity limits employment opportunities and increases health care costs. There is a 42% obesity rate among welfare recipients.

No direct housing aid should be given. Individuals, parents, and relatives could receive tax deductions and/or stipends for housing poor people. All direct aid government-housing programs would end. Parents might be a little more concerned when their 14-year-old daughter gets pregnant, when they know her, the baby and the baby's pseudo daddy are still going to be living in the same house with them.

When hurricane Katrina hit New Orleans, it was clearly a horrible disaster. Hundreds died and billions of dollars in damage was done. Thousands of helpless poor people were dislodged from their decrepit surroundings and moved to new mobile homes away from the neighborhood drug dealers and prostitutes. Eventually, many were moved to other cities, left their bad habits behind, found jobs, and created new and better lives.

This forced exodus was clearly beneficial to many people. Lesson learned until direct aid can be phased out the Government should routinely move those on welfare far enough where they are forced to start anew. Away from the people and places that have condemned them to poverty, drugs, and crime.

Summary actions to reduce the number of poor:

• Do not allow poverty level unwed mothers raise their newborn children.

• Relocate those on welfare to a different state every 3 years

• Phase out housing aid for welfare recipients and offer incentives to relatives and friends to provide housing.

• Develop activities that require those on welfare to develop a pattern like employed people getting up early going to work and so on.

A wise associate liked to point out that, "People repeat what they like and don't repeat what they don't like." Mental and physical comfort is the virus that eventually overcomes the poor, making them incapable of changing their lives. The poor learn what is required to exist and see their lifestyle as the norm. They call government money they are given a paycheck and they fall into a comfortable pattern where years go by and any opportunities for self-improvement are lost to hanging out, alcohol, drugs, potato chips, and game shows.

I believe what Benjamin Franklin was saying is, you are not going to reduce the number of poor by giving them things others work for. The question is, do you want happy poor people or fewer poor people?

Chapter 2

Crime

"In October 2013, the incarceration rate of the United States of America was the highest in the world, at 716 per 100,000 of the national population. While the United States represents about 4.4 percent of the world's population, it houses around 22 percent of the world's prisoners. Corrections (which includes prisons, jails, probation, and parole) cost around $74 billion in 2007 according to the **U.S. Bureau of Justice Statistics."**

Many remember the days when a person could take an evening walk, leave a car unlocked, and leave the doors and windows open on a hot night. Today we all spend part of our time and money avoiding crime. Locking doors, setting alarms, staying indoors, avoiding evening activities, moving to new locations, changing to a safer driving route and collectively spending billions of dollars on crime prevention systems. We are no longer really free in our own homes and neighborhoods. What has changed? Many things, but law enforcement people will tell you, its drugs. They say, 99% of crime is drug-related.

Drug addicts commit crime 255 days a year!

The day to-day criminality of heroin addicts in Baltimore — A study in the continuity of offense rates

"A representative sample of 354 male heroin addicts living in the Baltimore metropolitan area was traced from onset of opiate use to time of interview to ascertain any changes in the frequency or type of offences committed during their years at risk."

"Five basic measures of criminality were employed: crime-day theft, crime-day violence, crime-day dealing, crime-day con games and crime-day other

*offences. A sixth measure —
composite crime day —
incorporated all five crime-day
measures. Crime rates per year
were derived from these six
measures."*

*"It was found that the start of
addiction was associated with a
high level of criminality (255
composite crime-days per year),
and that this high rate continued
over numerous subsequent
periods of addiction. Theft of
property was the most common
type of crime, followed by drug
sales, other offences, con games,
and violent offences."*

John C. Ball, John W. Shaffer, David N. Nurco

At this writing, over 2.2 million people are
incarcerated in the USA at an estimated cost of
$30,000 per year. It's a revolving door 9,000,000
are released and millions more go in every year.

People always have a choice not to commit a
crime. Even though, the media glamorize the
gangster lifestyle and no matter how routine it

appears, crime is always a choice. Do not be tempted to rationalize crime because of poverty, bad neighborhoods and bad schools these things surely exist but crime is always a choice. I repeat; crime is always a choice

"Cape Cod police officer, 32, is shot in the head and killed while serving an arrest warrant by a career criminal who had 111 prior offenses"

Mirror

It is obvious that our current legal system is not a deterrent. In addition, most crimes go totally unpunished because of the sheer number or legally swept under the table through plea-bargaining. Jail is more of a place to stay until the criminal incentive subsides. My view is that many young people choose a life of crime because they are prosecuted for just a small percentage of their crimes. Many join the rampant criminal gangs that require committing crimes to maintain membership. It appears to the irrational young that crime actually pays. Criminal life becomes their occupation. This is not just a problem for the USA. Recent news out of England indicated only 9% of crimes are solved in large portions of the country.

Imagine committing a crime 255 days a year, obviously, most of those crimes go unpunished. This pattern, commit a batch of crimes a little jail time, commit a batch of crimes a little jail time, repeats until the criminal' either dies or loses the energy to keep up with the younger guys coming up.

Notice the direct link of drug use to drug dealing. Drug addicts steal to buy drugs. With the money, they hope to buy more drugs then they can use so they can sell the excess at a profit to buy more drugs. Walmart by virtue of its size may be one of the largest sources of illegal drug money. Drug addicts shoplift millions of dollars in merchandise to pay for their drug habit. Customers, of course, pay more for products to offset the loss.

Those that actually end up in prison are most likely to be habitual criminals that have committed more serious crimes before they are imprisoned. Currently, the legal system does all it can to avoid incarcerating criminals. Space is limited and the imprisoned are almost certain to commit more crimes when released. Also, those that have reached prison have proven to the courts that their criminal life has reached a level that has no chance of being reversed.

Jail serves as the criminal's higher education where degrees with majors in breaking and entering, shoplifting, firearms, con games and robbery are granted to all. The only way to reduce the recidivism rate is to stop the criminal behavior early. Otherwise, the criminal habits persist and the possibility of the individual contributing to society is lost. Obviously, a thirty-year-old with a drug habit and a prison record is going have a very tough time. In this case, an ounce of prevention is worth millions of pounds of cure. We have to stop this criminal way of life before it starts.

According to United States Department of Justice:

• 69% of felons have multiple prior arrests.

• 49% of felons have multiple convictions.

• 35% of those charged with felonies have 10 or more prior arrests and another   17% have between 5 to 9 arrests, thus 52% of charged felons have been arrested and before the courts many times.

• 40% of those charged with burglary and motor vehicle theft have 10 or more arrests.

Am I the only one that sees a problem with this? Shouldn't we be trying to prevent criminal behavior before it becomes a habit? How long are we going to sit and watch this continue?

According to the Justice Center:

• 30% of violent offenders have 10 or more prior arrests.

• Federal and state corrections facilities held over 1.6 million prisoners at the end of 2010 — approximately one of every 201 U.S. residents.

• Approximately 9 million individuals are released from prison each year. (A high percentage of jail sentences are less than a year)

• Over 6 million of those returning from prison have a history of substance use disorders.

• Nearly 4.9 million individuals were on probation or parole at the end of 2010.

50,000 here, 700,000 there, 2,900,000 in, 9,000,000 out, 5,000,000 on probation, pretty soon that's going to be a BIG NUMBER!

In a study that looked at recidivism in over 40 states, more than 40% of offenders returned to state prison within three years of their release.

In 2009, parole violators accounted for 33.1% of all prison admissions, 35.2% of state admissions, and 8.2% of federal admissions.

23% of adults ending parole in 2010 – 127,918 individuals – returned to prison because of violating their terms of supervision, and 9% of adults ending parole in 2010 - 49,334 individuals - returned to prison because of a new conviction.

If communities could afford more police officers, The number incarcerated would be much larger. More police more prisoners, is that a good goal for society?

In addition, a high percentage of the 500,000 homeless are mentally ill drug addicted or both. The incidence of serious mental illnesses is two to four times higher among prisoners than it is in the general population.

In a study of more than 20,000 adults entering five local jails, researchers documented serious mental illnesses in 14.5% of the men and 31% of the women, which taken together, comprises 16.9% of those studied — rates more than three to six times those found in the general population.

The cost of caring for the mentally ill would be nominal compared to the overall cost of maintaining our giant prison system at its current level. Imagine the quality of care we could provide the mentally ill if we reduced the crime rate by 90%.

When assessing the massive amount of crime in the US we should not overlook the negative effect crime has on children. Studies show the first 3 years of development are very important to the attitudes about education and future success of a child. Interactions with their fathers also affect success. The children of couples that fight and or experience trauma may have lower IQ's and be more likely to fail in school. Imagine, how many children's lives would be better if we could reduce the crime rate by 90%?

"Many people inside prisons lack education. Dropout rates are seven times greater for children in impoverished areas than those who come from families of higher incomes. This is due to the fact that many children in poverty are more likely to have to work and care for family members. People in prisons generally come from poverty

*creating a continuous cycle of
poverty and incarceration."*

wikipedia.org

Another indirect negative result of rampant crime is its effect on how children are raised in families not directly associated with crime. Studies (Winterbottom, M. R., et.al.) show early independence training can positively affect how a child manages growing up and dealing with life's issues. Early Independence Training includes early exposure to learning to tie shoes, crossing the street by one's self, and so on. Early independence can reduce a child's fear of failure. Which can be a valuable asset in adult life.

A result of the high crime rate is that parents fear for their child's safety and hover over their kids preventing them from learning to do activities on their own. Recently, some parents were arrested for letting their children play in a park and walk home by themselves. When I was a kid, I left the house in the morning, returned home when my mom came and got me after the street lights came on at night. There do not appear to be any benefits from growing up in fear.

I propose adopting this 3F-50/50 Penalty to prosecute those who choose crime:

3F- 50/50 Penalty

• All felonies count 1 point.

• Felonies, which result in a death, count 2 points.

• By Federal law within 4 hours of conviction, felons who accumulate three or more felony points would be required by law to push a button on a machine that can end life based on 50/50 odds. Each felony over three would require an additional 3F- 50/50 Penalty. If this procedure does not result in the death of the habitual felon, the felon would serve the usual prison time as administered by the courts.

During the four-hour waiting period following conviction, the convicted felon could reduce 3F-50/50 felony points by providing information that would solve significant crimes and avoid the 3F-50/50 penalty process.

If this system were enacted, there would be no opportunity for appeal prior to the 3F-50/50 Penalty procedure. Do not forget this is the individual's third felony conviction. We are not dealing with rookie criminals or first-time offenders. They have repeatedly chosen crime and most crimes are never prosecuted. If the repeat offender survives the 3F-50/50 process, they could still appeal their case. The goal of 3F-50/50 is to prevent a life of crime before it starts.

The enactment of the 3F-50/50 penalty law would result in a huge reduction in serious crime in the USA. Far fewer people, both victim, and criminal would die because there would be far fewer criminal acts. Relatively few felons would actually lose their lives to the 3F-50/50 penalty, as they would know life as a criminal is short. They would need to find another career. To cause a death during a crime could potentially risk their own life to the 3F-50/50 penalty.

As the crime rate dropped so would illegal drug use. Criminals know that their drug addiction leads to crime, so they would take more advantage of substance abuse programs. In addition, felons could trade 3F-50/50 points for evidence toward convicting drug dealers.

Millions of men spend what would be there working and child-rearing years in prison. Imagine if instead of prison, they were even moderately educated and say, just 50% entered the workforce.

Instead of absorbing tax dollars, those would be criminals would be taxpayers. We are talking about millions of men. There would have to be fewer unwed mothers just from a purely statistical standpoint of more available men.

In 2013, there were 33,000 firearm deaths. 11 thousand of those were homicides (murder). The perceived threat from the high crime rate encourages gun ownership and resultant deaths.

According to the American Journal of Medicine. *"Overall, our results show that the U.S., which has the most firearms per capita in the world, suffers disproportionately from firearms compared with other high-income countries," said* **study author Erin Grinshteyn**, *an assistant professor at the School of Community Health Science at the University of Nevada-Reno. "These results are consistent with the hypothesis that our firearms are killing us rather than protecting us,"*

Gun ownership, accidental gun deaths and suicides would decline in the USA as the perceived need for a weapon for security would decline. There would also be the reality that a weapon caused death could be interpreted as a crime because of the gun owner's faulty judgment which would count as two felony points and lead to the 3F-50/50 Penalty and death. Individuals with previous felony convictions would realize any association with a deadly weapon could mean a 50/50 chance of death.

Sadly, the illegal drug industry flourishes, providing jobs and income for millions of people. I suspect many people would not qualify for government assistance if they were to report their income from selling drugs. Drug money flows just like any other commercial enterprise, ending up as church donations and liquor store purchases. Many will want to hold on to their drug-related jobs.

Because of the widespread illegal drug trade, the adoption of the 3F-50/50 penalty law would create a backlash at first. The black community would say it is racial discrimination and so on. Others would say it is cruel. As would the drug infested entertainment industry. However, when the crime-ridden communities started to see the peace and calm in their neighborhoods with money and investments coming their way they would change their attitude and support it.

It just dawned on me, that this could be the first opportunity in our Nation's history that all black Americans could live normal lives as promised in the Constitution. I have to believe that a disproportionate number of affected black citizens are sick and tired of dealing with poverty, drugs, crime, and murder. In the end, trillions of dollars could be redirected from law enforcement to education and mental health care. What a wonderful thought.

Related to the crime problem is the number of women that are stalked, abused, murdered by ex-husbands and boyfriends. This behavior seems to be growing as rarely a day passes that some rejected male doesn't kill his wife and sometimes his children.

I believe the rejected males thought processes get stuck repeating themselves like a record with a scratch. Playing the same destructive thoughts over and over again. I would like to see a study conducted where males who exhibit this behavior are given ECT Electro Convulsive Therapy. Better known and electroshock therapy, it has had its critics over the years. But it is still being used because it works. It has been very helpful to the severely depressed. Depression I believe is similar in its effect on the individual's repetitive thought processes as the rejected male who cannot stop thinking about his situation. Scientists are not a 100% sure how ECT actually works but it has the effect of spinning back the memory and feelings before the depression began. I would like to see if a course of ECT could reduce the number of murders and suicides by male partners.

Chapter 3

Education

If educations' primary objective is gainful employment, shouldn't the high school curriculum reflect the needs of employers? Below are the skills and traits every employer wants their employees to know.

Employer's hire and reward

• Critical Thinking: Seeing the big picture and being analytical; comprehending what you read.

• Communication: Getting your point across effectively when writing and speaking.

• Visionary Qualities: Brainstorming, looking to the future, setting goals.

• Self-Motivation: Showing a willingness to take the initiative.

• Proficiency with Information: Being inquisitive, curious and resourceful, knowing how to conduct research.

• Globally Minded: Understanding and showing an interest in other cultures and getting along with diverse groups of people.

• Teamwork: Working well with others to achieve common goals.

Desired Traits Employers want to see in an employee:

• Being dependable.

• Pulling together a presentation.

• Solving problems.

• Coaching co-workers.

• Fitting into the company's culture.

• Voicing opinions while being open to feedback.

• Being flexible and focused.

• Being creative and innovative.

• Developing new work processes.

• Taking initiative.

• Strong Work Ethic

• Positive Attitude

- Time Management Abilities

- Problem-Solving Skills

- Acting as a Team Player

- Self-Confidence

- Ability to Accept and Learn From Criticism

- Flexibility/Adaptability

- Working Well Under Pressure

Notice they do not mention algebra, geography, music, art, and the other traditional subjects' high schools offer.

You might ask how I can be so sure about what kids need to study to get a job. Well, I spent a large part of my years as a college administrator studying job demands analyzing skills required and designing college degree programs. Early in my career, I developed a knack for identifying and designing college programs that were ahead of their time and on target for the job market. Our college had a history of preparing people for jobs, well before it became popular because students were acquiring huge student loans and had to have jobs to pay them off.

Over the last 15 years or so, all of the student grants and easy student loan programs gave colleges a "license to kill", so to speak. The student loan programs allowed tuition to be raised to unbelievable heights. Yet parents were so happy their kid was going to college, they encouraged them to sign papers of indebtedness, which in their unrealistic dreams thought somehow would mysteriously be paid.

The cost of college needs to be lowered so a middle-income family can afford it without going into major debt. Various free tuition schemes have been tried with little success. College without some sacrifice has never been successful.

Many colleges and universities are just like bloated government agencies full of bureaucratic email shuffling personnel and tenured faculty flying around the world to this meeting and that conference. Many tenured college professors would feign death to avoid teaching a class. All the while students are going deeper into debt. A great college education does not have to cost as much as it does today.

There are two pseudo-facts that affect the cost of education but not learning, class size and age or condition of classrooms. Many studies show larger class sizes are actually better learning environments than small classes. Studies find kids in large classes learn from each other. Teachers striking over 5 or 10 more kids in a class will have no bearing on how much those kids will actually learn.

In addition, students will learn just as much in a barn or an architectural edifice. All you need to do is look at a school in Bangladesh. The teacher's level of enthusiasm and subject knowledge are the primary reasons students learn, no matter the size of the class or condition of the building.

My bible was the Occupational Outlook Handbook published by the Department of Labor every 2 years (https://www.bls.gov/ooh/). The Handbook lists all the recognized occupations in the United States including education required and expected job demand. A must read if you have a child getting ready for college. My friends and I will jokingly say some parents have Histaphobia. That is a fear their child will major in History. Implying, of course, there is not much of a job demand for History majors.

I would like to require colleges to have student and parent sign an acknowledgment that they have read and understand the cost of education, student loan payments amount per month, interest paid, penalties for nonpayment, job and income prospects, history of loan repayment for the chosen college's graduates of this curriculum for the field of study their child has selected.

Income has a high correlation with educational levels. In 2007, the median earnings of a household headed by individuals with less than a 9th-grade education was $20,805 while households headed by high school graduates earned $40,456, households headed by holders of bachelor's degrees earned $77,605, and families headed by individuals with professional degrees earned $100,000.

Our current educational system is designed to weed out when it should be weeding in. The high school diploma is a ticket to the next level in all phases of life.

- The high school diploma is a ticket to college.

- The high school diploma is a ticket to a job.

- The high school diploma is a ticket to self-esteem.

Those without a diploma are pretty much-assured unemployment, welfare, and or prison. Surprisingly as a nation, we do not seem too concerned about annually writing off 600,000 youth who do not graduate from high school and are almost assured failure. Think of it, 6 million people every 10 years. The lack of a diploma will be a drag on their success and happiness all their lives. How can we condemn children who are measured by ancient values and useless criteria?

"DC's public schools have gone from a point of pride to one of the city's largest embarrassments

The internal investigation concluded that more than one-third of the 2017 graduating class should not have received diplomas due to truancy or improper steps taken by teachers or administrators to cover the absences. In one egregious example, investigators found that attendance records at Dunbar High School had been altered 4,000 times to mark absent students as present. The school system is now being investigated

Most high school graduates do not have any more knowledge than the kid who dropped out. Sad but true, colleges will tell you most high school graduates are not prepared for college. Remediation-style, starting from scratch, courses are commonplace in colleges today. Such as Math starting with number recognition as in counting 1 to 10 and English with learning the ABC's. Do not forget these are high school graduates. Currently, non-high school graduates cannot be accepted by colleges.

*"The number of kids in this
country who get to be juniors and
seniors in high school and think
that they're on track to be
successful in college, and they're
not even close, it's
heartbreaking," Duncan told
reporters after his speech. "It's*

*absolutely unfair when kids play
by all the rules and do all the
right things and still find out
they're not anywhere near where
they need to be."*

**Education Secretary Arne
Duncan**

Most high school students have a hard time relating to what they are being taught. Subjects are either clearly out of sync with the real world like algebra or useless time wasters like drama and dance. Dance is one of those things nice to know and offered by the high schools to keep kids interested. Job demand for professional dancers is minuscule compared to the huge number of applicants. In addition, I do not think I would want my daughter dancing half-naked for a drugged-up rapper in a music video. Like I said a waste of time.

Today, involvement with cell phones, computer games, social media, and electronic gadgets make it hard to get a kid's attention. Everyday school must be like going back in time for most kids. Imagine a high school experience that offers faster moving meaningful activities that kids know they are going to use plus a plane trip to a foreign country   Imagine kids looking forward to schooling!

Most teachers will tell you that kids are pretty-good learners until about the ages of 12 to 14. At that time kid's hormones or something, take over that makes them harder to handle and teach. I would suggest that we start as early as possible to begin to teach reading, writing, math, and science. I would say about the age of three. I believe kids can learn information that is much more complex then we have traditionally expected. Kids think everything is fun. Therefore, we can make foreign language, math and science fun in the early stages, especially. Eventually, more complex math and science can be introduced. In Taiwan, they teach calculus in the 7th grade.

You will notice the subjects I recommend being offered in elementary through 8th grade are foreign language, reading, writing, Math, and Science. That is because all people must have at least a minimum level of knowledge to function in society. The simplest jobs in the United States require reading, basic math, and basic science. Today, even a janitor must be able to read labels and be able to recognize cleaning chemicals that should not be mixed together. We owe all citizens that much as the educational bare minimum. Until all students meet or exceed grade level, spending valuable school time on anything else is criminal. Until students can demonstrate a minimum level of competency, they should not move on to High School.

Many will say they cannot imagine elementary and junior high without music and art. Music and art are fine, but only the naturally gifted musician or artist will have a slim chance to earn a living from those talents in adult life. All kids will benefit from being able to read and write. I find it interesting that parents will bend over backwards to have their child practice music and sports but not writing. Most people are not born writers it too requires practice. I would want children practicing writing in school a couple of hours every day. It will be so valuable to them in the future.

I would require all students to copy a book cover-to-cover, cursive or printing, not typed. I believe non-readers never practiced. Copying a 400-page book would dramatically improve reading and writing skill. I would recommend book subjects about inventors, scientists, people whose lives made a positive impact on the world.

"Despite investing heavily in early literacy since 2015, Michigan schools showed the largest decline in third-grade reading levels among 11 comparable states in the last three years, according to a new education report.

Because those 56 percent of third-graders did not pass the reading test on Michigan's state assessment in 2017, about 60,308 students would have faced being retained under Michigan's new reading law if the retention trigger was already in place.

*In the Detroit Public Schools Community District, the number of third-graders who scored proficient in reading on the M-STEP was 9.9 percent in 2017, meaning **more than 90 percent of students could not pass the test**."*

The Detroit News

It must be a goal of education to teach everyone to read and write with some level of competency. I believe there are millions of people in the United States that have spent years in school who still cannot read and write. It was not unusual to find autoworkers I was training who could not read. Surprisingly, while conducting training with elementary schools I found a few elementary teachers that had questionable reading ability, really.

Therefore, I say, we pour on math, science, reading and writing in the early years before the peer pressure and craziness gets to them. The goal for every kid would be to enter high school with a say, a minimum 6th-grade reading, math, and science level. Maybe with a shift to spending 3 or 4 hours reading and writing each day we could get that minimum level up to 7th or 8th grade. This is about the grade level large numbers of high school graduates have attained who graduate from the non-elite colleges and community colleges. I'm confident the college success rate would be much better if entering students were skilled at writing.

"The problem is not scientifically illiterate kids; it is scientifically illiterate adults. Kids are born

curious about the natural world.
They are always turning over
rocks, jumping with two feet into
mud puddles and playing with the
tablecloth and fine china." **Neil**
deGrasse Tyson

How did all this education get started? It began like this. Over hundreds of year's rulers, countries and philosophers developed a curriculum, which included subjects that wealthy people of the day thought were important to teach to their children. School required about 4 years. Many believe it was 4 years because education included travel, which required about a year for the students to travel to England or France and back, and so on.

All modern education stems from those early beginnings. Obviously, only the wealthy could afford to educate their children. Eventually, schools were built in villages and towns as skilled tradesmen and shop owners needed people who could calculate and keep records for the king's tax collectors.

At one time women were only taught to read. Only men were taught to both read and write.

Apparently, it was believed women did not have any thoughts worth writing down.

In the USA, interest groups have gathered data comparing students in the United States to other countries. As expected, the top 20% of American students compare well. The top 20% being classified as mostly white and Asian. Obviously, we are failing to help those who need education the most.

> ***Whatever happened to art classes at schools, Hong Kong parent asks – is it because the subject is not academic enough?***
>
> *South China Morning Post*

Elitist educators from the beginning of time felt that education should be what was called "well rounded". What they meant was that to be a "complete" human being you should not only know the practical things like math and English you should also know poetry, art, sciences. Supposedly, so a person could experience all life has to offer. That has been, I think, the ongoing problem with education the brightest people decided what and how something should be taught. Moreover, they cannot relate to the average person's learning needs or ability.

So today we offer high school subjects like, Algebra, English literature, calculus, airport management, history, geography, Hebrew, dance, drama, guitar, computer language, French, Latin, Chinese and the list goes on. Many classes appear to be offered to entertain in hopes the student will enjoy them enough to stay in school.

Sadly, in response to the arbitrary US educational system, we have millions of children being penalized for failing to learn information of questionable value, which condemns them to a life of low-level income and a high probability of criminal activity and drug use.

Nowadays in the typical high school classroom, information is presented by the teacher, sometimes as a lecture, sometimes in written form or with a variety of media. Many of you might remember having books in school. Today books are not used that much, especially in the intercity.

Books are expensive, and they are damaged and lost.

The teacher will explain and demonstrate what they think are the hard parts and answer questions. Sometime classes will be divided into groups or teams. The teacher tells the student what is important in the information and may have the student practice the information.

After a time, a few days or weeks, the student's memory will be tested on what the teacher, State, and Federal Government believe is important and give the student a grade. I admit this is a broad generalization. I do know that all teachers teach differently. My own college teacher education did not direct me to teach in a specific manner. It pretty much implied do it the way I thought was best.

Most teacher education today includes exposure to widely accepted learning methods, which may have some value. It's the future teacher's option to use them or not. Enthusiasm, the trait that all great traditional teachers must have, cannot be taught.

How much a student will learn is dependent on how much the teacher knows about the subject

and how enthusiastic they are when teaching the subject.

It seems like knowledge and enthusiasm should go hand and hand. However, a teacher that has a Ph.D. in math may not be able to sell the benefits of math to the student. Not all the math knowledge in the world will help a teacher who cannot enthusiastically convince the student math should be important to them, also.

Many states now require teachers to take a qualifying exam before they can teach school. The test is a positive step, but it does not indicate whether a person will be a good teacher. It is doubtful the best teachers were very effective in their first few years on the job. Since there are thousands of first-time teachers every year, there are many more thousands of kids that are "Guinea pigs" getting a mediocre education at best while new teachers learn their trade.

Over the years, I have asked many people if they had any enthusiastic teachers that really knew their subject well. Most say something like, "Oh yes, Mrs. Audrey in 9th grade. She taught English." Most people can only think of one, sometimes two. Sadly, I did not have one of those great teachers.

My problem is this; shouldn't we all be able to list several great teachers we had in the past? This is just more proof the educational system based on teachers passing on information does not work.

"There are many things that go into developing a good instructor. Many of these things are a matter of style. Those things aside, there are three things that all good instructors have at their core - enthusiasm, subject knowledge, and preparation. If you can master these three elements, everything else is gravy."

Ask the Dean Jim Rohn

In addition to enthusiasm, we are unrealistic to believe all teachers have a high level of subject knowledge. In many cases, a high school teacher is only required to have one college-level course such as algebra to teach an algebra class in high school.

If we were in the teacher's lounge might we hear, "How do they expect me to be fired up, rah, rah, rah every day?" Exactly, we are unrealistic to expect teachers to be enthusiastic-- fired up every day. Yet that is what our current system of education requires to be truly successful. We are expecting teachers to do the impossible.

More knowledgeable teachers, new schools, more money, more testing none of these efforts have made a difference. If we were to increase these things tenfold, it still would not make a difference. All will be solved when the student believes school is worth the effort. Students are the customers, not the parents, not the teachers, not the colleges, not the government and a truth as old as time holds true today. The customer is always right.

The **EXPERIENCED BASED** approach to education I propose had its beginnings in the early 1970's. Competition in America from foreign manufacturers was growing. Civil rights, title 9, QWL Quality of Work Life, Quality Circles, Team Development, Statistical Process Control and The Right to Know Law, were collectively having an impact on corporate America. At the same time, computer technology was entering every phase of business and manufacturing. All these things required employee training.

During this time, organizations like the American Society for Training and Development were supporting trainers and corporate training departments who were under pressure to deliver employee training. The style of training that was the most effective was to create experiences that the employee could easily relate to and transfer to their office or factory job.

For example, here is a high school level question that might be asked after experiencing a session in Team Building.

What should your team do if two members of your team do not agree?

#1 take a vote to decide who is right

#2 involve the team in a discussion and come to an agreement.

#3 have the two members leave the room to discuss it and return with their answer.

The correct answer is #2, involve the team in a discussion and come to an agreement.

#1 to vote, forces the teams to take sides which hinders teamwork.

#3 to take the disagreement outside, whatever the two disagreeing members decide is not likely to be supported by all the team members and lead to bigger problems later.

You are probably asking how is this different from what is being done in schools today. The difference is that student groups or teams would participate in specially designed experiences that help them realize that #2 is the correct answer. Rather than being required to read a chapter or listen to a teacher and hope the student remembered what they heard or what they read.

With **EXPERIENCED BASED EDUCATION (EBE),** people learn almost without realizing it. Facts are not read, displayed or lectured about, instead what students experience, see and feel helps them come to the correct conclusions. You might think of EBE as full body memory experience involving all the senses, which tends to help a person recall and use the knowledge.

Have you ever been daydreaming a bit while driving? Maybe without thinking decide to make a left turn and out of nowhere, a truck with horn blaring zooms by. Your first thought after your heart starts beating again is, Yip! I'm not going to do that again. That's experience-based learning.

Imagine you wanted to learn to play golf. However, you did not have golf clubs or a ball, only a how-to golf book. No matter how many times you read the book you really could not say you knew how to golf. With EBE, education situations are created that actually; mimic the real job interactions and tasks, as in the real thing.

EBE has an advantage over traditional teaching methods. The EBE facilitator mostly makes sure that the students understand the instructions to the experience. The more students learn on their own the better. The students should get good results even if the EBE facilitator is not enthusiastic-- "fired up every day."

I knew many teachers. Moreover, I believe that they were absolutely sure they were doing the right thing. They worked so hard and really cared about their students. Many teachers will say to stop all of this government-sponsored student testing and evaluation. They say, "I did not learn to be a teacher for all of this hassle. Leave me alone and just let me teach. I know what to do."

Today, meaningful changes in education are impossible to make as everyone teaches the same subject a different way at a different time. Any attempts at changes in this structure are fought by independent teachers who have guaranteed jobs. All teachers think their way is best, yet they are terrified they might be compared to another teacher. So, they never venture far from their Teacher's Union security blanket.

Actually, teachers would be better off if testing and evaluation were implemented years ago. The reason teachers are in such trouble is even after 200 years or so of teaching kids in US schools we still don't know what to teach and the best way to teach it.

One year in Michigan a new high school was brought online which changed the previously racially separated districts to a more balanced racial mix. In addition, many teachers were transferred to accommodate the redistricting. One day I had occasion visit a teacher after her classes. I asked the (white) teacher about how things were going in the new high school. Tears began to trickle down her face as she described her frustration with her now mostly black student class. She said, "You can't teach these (black) kids anything".

Her response was something I never forgot. Because she believed, black students were incapable of learning. Moreover, I do not think her beliefs were unique. I suspect there are thousands of teachers that feel the same way. How do we expect black students to achieve when their teachers do not believe they are capable of learning?

If you are a schoolteacher, you are probably pretty mad at me by now. I am sorry you are offended. However, what you are doing as a group is not working for a large number of students. Only the most intelligent and motivated students learn and benefit from a typical high school education. The other 80% do not get much "bang for their buck."

Why do I say 80% do not get what they need? Studies indicate, only the top 20% of high school graduates compare well with students from other advanced countries. This means 80% of high school graduates are getting something less. Another way to look at it is, the smart kids do well and learn a lot and the average kids don't.

How many AP credits a high school's graduates test out of is not a measure of success. We have 2 million people in prison something has to change.

Be aware, that when business and industry train people they cannot flunk out 30%. Their students are employees. Therefore, the training has to be 100% effective. If not, the trainer/teacher loses their job, not the employee/student. I have to laugh at colleges and high schools that brag about how well their high-test score graduates fair. That is no accomplishment. That's like helping Eskimos adapt to cold weather. When the low and average ability students are successful, that is something to brag about.

Studies show that teachers that have the highest degree of subject knowledge and enthusiasm have the highest achieving students.

> *"The enthusiasm of the teacher is the key for a good learning in school. This arouses the student interest, maintains his attention and positive attitude. In this way, there is an increase in student motivation, which influences the performance, good results obtained by the student in the learning process."*

About 20% of teachers are enthusiastic combined with a high amount of subject knowledge. This assures high school kids that 80% of their teachers are not the best.

The famous quality guru Edwards Deming had proven that the best person to train a new employee is the manager/supervisor, not another worker. The worker is more likely to unintentionally, pass on methods that lead to lower quality. Similarly, a high school teacher, (worker) learn subjects from college professors (management/supervisor) and take what they think is important and pass it on to the student. Definitely not what Mr. Deming would have condoned?

Colleges should be the experts and pass on the specific occupationally related knowledge directly, while high schools teach the employment-related and interpersonal skills that both high school and a college graduate will need to be successful on the job.

Many colleges and their faculty are offended by the term "occupational" in connection with student outcomes. Educational elitists feel college is a place to explore one's intellect. If the student is both independently wealthy and a genius that might be fine. However, I have always felt that the goal of any college program of study should be meaningful employment.

I know there are colleges and college professors that believe they are above all that, but they do not serve the average graduate well. Who, after high school graduation finds he no longer likes living with his parents and would like to move away from home. Higher Education does not seem to care if the student's money and time are wasted. Maybe they are the greedy "fat cats" politicians are referring too.

"The share of American young adults living with their parents is the highest in 75 years"

"Parents in the US cannot get rid of their kids. The share of young adults in their late 20s living with

*their parents is the highest it's
been in 75 years. According to a
recent study by the **Pew Research
Center**, 33% of 25-29 year olds
lived with their parents or
grandparents in 2016. This is
almost three times as many as in
1970."*

Employers say they want people who can work in a team, recognize what needs to be done, have initiative, and good social skills. Colleges teach few if any of these extremely important interpersonal skills. In addition, college students do not want to spend the high costs of college tuition and time on classes that are not related to their college major. High school is where kids should learn these important interpersonal skills.

During my research of job interview skills of applicants in typical blue-collar jobs in industry, I found it was not unusual for the job applicant not say a word. <u>Not hello, not yes, not no, not a word!</u> In my idea of experienced-based high school curriculum, all students would shake hands with a greeting a thousand times a school year. Therefore, a handshake, smile and a greeting would become a useful habit.

Susan, an Expert in Emotional and Physical Growth points out,

> *"Children with poor socialization skills are less likely to form healthy intimate relationships as adults, more likely to experience peer rejection, and have a higher likelihood of running into trouble either with the juvenile or adult legal system. Social skills in schools impact safety as well as interpersonal interactions because students with poor social skills are more likely to demonstrate aggressive or violent behavior, are less likely to be able to self-regulate their behavior and have trouble asking or accepting help from others, which makes violence a more likely response to conflicts."*

The teen years are a perfect time when socializing skills can be learned. Traditional high school education does not always lend itself to learning to work together or depend on another for help and coordination of effort. Most teens are not ready to apply themselves to the subjects of questionable value high schools offer. Generally, important interpersonal skills are learned at the expense of the first employer who either teaches them or fires new workers because they do not exhibit them.

Colleges have reduced class time requirements over the years. As they reduced class time, they have had better completion rates. Actually, the federal government finally had to step in and set standards because many colleges were not requiring even a minimal level of class attendance.

High school should be shortened to 3 years. Students will stay with it when they can see the end is in sight. In addition, most states mandate that a student must stay in school until the age of 16. Many of those 16-year-old dropouts would now qualify for a high school diploma.

Educators routinely claim that a school is only as good as the level of parental involvement. So, let us think about this. What level of parental involvement should we expect from single or no parent households in intercity Detroit, Chicago, Los Angeles, and intercity America? The success of our educational system should not depend on parental involvement.

What subjects do high school students need to learn? I do not think anyone could possibly know that answer. From the earliest of times, the smartest people guessed what they thought the masses should know. Currently, I do not know anyone who uses algebra accepts an algebra teacher. Many things are nice to know. I think that is why many kids have problems in school they know they are not likely to use what the school is trying to teach them. A goal for high school education should be that when a graduate reaches retirement age they could look back and identify specific things they learned that they used during their working career.

Should we be comparing our educational goals to other countries? Why do we care if Swedish kids learn algebra? Facts are we do not know what kids will need when it comes to specific subject knowledge. Chances are we all know someone who is successfully working in a field not even close to their major studies in college. We do know it will be beneficial to be able to work in teams get along with all people including those from other countries and be ready for the opportunities that life offers.

I wonder does the average person ever need to study advanced math. Unless you are a scientist, the entire math you are ever going to use is readily available on your cell phone. Technology makes everything easier. When I first learned to drive a car, I had to shift gears, steer the car, and stick my arm out the window to signal a turn. Soon there will be cars that will only require the ability to sit. Recently, California decided to give cars a driver's license. "Honest officer, I did not park the car here. The car thought this was a good spot."

In the 50's when I was in high school most of the people in my class knew, they could get a job in "the factory" and make $100 a week. You could live like a king on that kind of money. At that time, I was making 63 cents an hour in a grocery store. Moreover, I could buy a burger, fries, and a soda for 35 cents. Later, as a college educator, I worked with trainers in the auto industry where half of the assembly line workers did not have high school diplomas.

I do not know what the assembly line worker's high school graduate percentage level is today, but I am sure the total number of assembly line workers is down 70% or more. Michigan high school kids will likely never have the opportunity to work on a factory assembly line. They are going to need a high school diploma. In addition, they like all high school students are going to need to know how to function in a high-tech world.

The future of manufacturing and services will surely be changing. It does not make sense to equip a high school with the latest expensive technical equipment only to have it be out of date in a few years. Colleges, like it or not, are finding they are being rated based on the successful employment of their graduates. It makes sense that colleges should have the latest equipment and methods employers use. High schools will never be able to keep up with the rapid changes in high tech equipment. With colleges having the latest equipment the educational system, will only pay for the equipment once during the lifetime of the technology. High school education should be about personal development, which is not equipment intensive and inherently lower in cost. During my years employed in education, I formed close relationships with high school counselors and related counseling groups. Something that bothered me was their approach to career counseling. Firstly, I think by the time a student finishes high school they should know the careers for which they are best suited. High School counselors were fearful of telling a student what career they should choose.

The theory was, give the student career surveys and counseling but never tell the student what to do. Always let the student decide. In theory that seems OK. The problem is many students are unrealistic and or cannot make up their mind and do not make a commitment to do anything. Kids do not always know what is best for them. They leave high school with unrealistic expectations or wander without a plan. I think it is better for a young person to be pointed in a career direction than to not start at all.

Designed properly, EBE will assure all students know their best career choices and they will have a plan to achieve success in a specific career path. I picture high school students with name tags to encourage career planning that includes a job title...Leticia Johnson, Electrical Engineer, Matt Wilson, Medical Technician.

I suppose many people will say that changing to an experience-based approach where all you have to do is participate is just "dumbing down" school. Not so, I assure you. You really cannot use terms like, easy or hard to describe EBE those words do not apply. All students will understand the purpose of what they are doing. Some students who eventually graduate from college might use what they have learned to manage people while those going directly to work might use the same knowledge to better understand job responsibilities and get along better with fellow workers.

There are many benefits to a college degree such as higher income, longer life, longer marriage, better health and so on. However, I believe high school emphasis on college is ill-advised. Only about 35% of working age people have a 2-year degree or more. In good economic times, we could use more college graduates, but reality shows we are getting along on the current number pretty well. 69% of high school graduates start college and about 48% of those that start **DO NOT** graduate. That leaves a huge number of people who have spent time and money in college with nothing to show for it. Only the colleges benefit from this.

 Seems like we should be able to do a better job of guidance and evaluation before we encourage someone to go to college. I believe college dropouts do gain some important knowledge, improved basic skills such as, how to read, their best occupational choice, and so on. College is expensive, and this knowledge should have been acquired in free public K-12 school. Seems like colleges have scholarships backwards they should offer the first year free to those with average test scores. They are the ones who need the help.

Today for 80% of students, high school is a waste of time. It does not help them get a job and it does not prepare them for college. Remember, EBE is going to educate the student, also. It is just going to do it in a different and more effective way. EBE will teach the student skills that will help them go directly to either work or college.

When the job market is good, more high school graduates tend to go directly to work and not go to college. When the job market is depressed, they realize college is a good idea and more kids go to college. Currently, colleges expect incoming students to have skills in English and math. The problem is most high school graduates do not acquire competence in English and math.

Conversely, EBE high school graduates that have been employed will have those things they learned in high school reinforced on the job. College programs in response to EBE would not expect older returning students to have English and math levels any different from a recent high school graduate. The college curriculum could build English and math skills as necessary to accommodate both past and recent high school graduates equally.

With the EBE model, almost 100% of the population will have a high school diploma. This will not only open more employment doors it will add much-needed self-confidence. Many adults fear going to college because they think recent high school graduates will know so much more than they do. Therefore, EBE will also keep the college door open and not discourage those who consider college later in life. Since they will know colleges always expect new students at a beginner level. Wise colleges will design their curriculum to build freshmen student's confidence and integrate EBE methods into their subject matter courses.

EBE changes the education process to be dependent on the student not on the teacher. It will transition most students not just the advantaged, into adulthood far better than high school does today. It will be exactly the same for every student. It will not be so dependent on the subject knowledge and enthusiasm of a teacher. It will minimize racial bias and assure a more equal opportunity for employment and or college for all students.

One of my responsibilities as a college administrator was managing graduate job search services (helping college graduates get jobs). Employers did not hesitate to tell us what they wanted in an employee. Getting along with others, seeing what needs to be done, teamwork, these are the types of things we should be sure our kids can do. Young people need to learn what is required to function in a work environment.

It makes sense that all students should have job seeking skills whether going directly into college or not. Most students need a job immediately after high school. In addition, many college students work at part-time jobs while in college and during breaks.

One of the EBE concepts that should be taught is how to apply for and get a job. One of the most successful techniques we taught was the 6-6-6 method. Talk to one employer every 6-day week for 6 weeks. Most graduates were employed after the second week.

According to the department of education 81% of 24-year-olds graduate from high school. What happened to 17 or 18 as the graduation age?

Actually, about 70% of Hispanics, American Indian and Blacks graduate in 4 years. There are about 1 million Hispanics, American Indians, and blacks in high school. This means that 300,000 Hispanics, American Indians, and blacks did not graduate. Not to mention another 300,000 whites. Therefore, it is obvious the kids we need to help the most are being helped the least.

Currently, our K-12 educational system does a great job of sorting the brightest from the average when the goal should be to prepare all for entry directly into the job market or college.

Colleges will have to change to adapt to graduates of EBE high school. Firstly, the freshmen class will not have taken an SAT or ACT. Freshmen could only be tested after acceptance. The college could only post the number of students they want in their freshmen class. The temptation might be "overbook" the class assuming a high dropout rate. However, I would recommend that the following year freshmen class numbers would be adjusted up or down depending on the previous year's success. I do not want colleges planning for dropouts. I prefer them to be planning for success. I will also bet that colleges would have many successful graduates that they would never have accepted under their old system.

Colleges will argue that they will not know if students are capable of college-level work without testing. Currently, half of all entering college freshmen do not graduate so what exactly is it they are claiming entry tests accomplish?

The traditional college curriculum will have to change as well. Over the years, colleges develop math departments, English departments, history departments, anyway so, lots of departments. Each department lobbies for required courses, needed or not. Currently, all the major college accrediting bodies require at least a semester of advanced level math. Where actually only a small number of careers require any advanced math knowledge.

We say a degree is earned. Maybe the earned part is struggling through a subject you hate and will never use. Again, that is all well and good until you consider the huge cost and how important the degree is to the student and the surrounding family. Many potential college students do not enroll for fear of these "struggle" subjects and many more drop out during the struggle. For example, thousands of people do not enroll and or graduate from college because of a speech class requirement. They are terrified to be in front of people. A semester of Speech 101 does not provide enough experience to make a difference. In reality, people rarely give speeches until they have acquired a volume of expertise. Sorry speech department.

The success ratio of today's high school student is determined by income, location, and race. The poorest usually African American populated intercity areas graduate the smallest percentage of students. One could assume even those that do graduate from high schools in these areas are not well prepared for work or college. EBE is an educational delivery system that is blind to the participant's race, financial or intelligence level. By its nature, it automatically adjusts to the status and educational level of the participants.

*The yearly study of child welfare
data, released Tuesday by the*

*Michigan League for Public Policy,
also found that 65 percent of
students aren't ready for college
or careers. Some 84 percent of
students from low-income
families aren't prepared
compared to 16 percent of
students from higher income
families."* **Detroit News**

I have personally trained hundreds of people using EBE methods. Groups varied from factory workers that did not finish high school to corporate officers and scientists some who had Ph.D.'s in Astronomy and Mathematics. I conducted the training the exact same way with the same materials and it was always well understood and evaluated highly successful by the employees of manufacturers, hospitals, banks, and schools, I trained.

Standardized EBE, focusing on the skills employers require, will be understood and valued by all levels of high school student. They will recognize the value and they will find EBE is more in tune with their interests and energy levels.

Although, EBE would have students conduct most of what they experience in teams. It would not necessarily mean students could only be successful if they worked on a team in real life. The reason teams are used for EBE is real job situations and employee interaction can be created easily when you work with groups.

There are other signs that EBE is needed. Many high schools today are very large with thousands of students. Building huge schools may bring the overall costs of education down but I do not think it is good for many kids. The kids I am concerned about are those that seem to get lost and do not adjust. High teen suicide rates and the Columbine massacre are extreme examples.

With EBE, students would be grouped randomly with a wide range of abilities and motivation. EBE by its nature brings people together. It makes them dependent on one another to achieve certain mutually beneficial goals. The students will be learning techniques of involving their fellow student team members. It will be much harder for an individual student to get lost in some fantasy world. Those students who have serious issues will be more easily recognized for referral to professionals for help.

The school day should be divided into experiences that provide the student with prescribed knowledge. Immediately following the prescribed experience, the student would complete an online survey. The results of which would immediately be recorded at a National Education Center and be made available via the internet. I picture something that has the look of the National Aeronautical and Space Administration in Huston, TX. Where educators would be watching giant displays seeing and evaluating education as it happens. Blast off!

If the EBE system was adopted, it would eliminate the homeschooling option as EBE requires students to be taught in groups. Isolation is the direct opposite of the purpose of EBE. So also, Charter Schools would likely not offer any advantage over the public-school system. Non-English-speaking students would find it much easier to adapt to team interaction.

All prescribed high school experiences would occur on the same day and hour as much as possible throughout the USA.

The reasons for having all the experiences taught on the same day and time include.

• Ease of measurement of the experience Student survey results would be available immediately following each classroom experience.

• Accommodates transferring students

 Parents, therefore, students are more mobile today. Students could easily transfer between schools even in another state, and not have to worry about which week of the semester it was or subject availability. The new student would actually add value to the teamwork training of EBE since real-world work teams have members come and go and the students will need to learn how to involve new team members.

> *"According to a 2009 report by the Calder Urban Institute with Duke University and five other institutions of higher learning,*

> *One in six of the nation's third-graders have attended at least three different schools since the beginning of the first grade, and student school mobility remains a common phenomenon at all school levels..."*

- EBE facilitator's mobility and flexibility

     Substituting for ill EBE facilitators would not affect the outcome. EBE facilitators could readily transfer all over the USA and quickly adapt to the standardized curriculum.

All learning would occur in the school during the school day. Homework would be rare. There would be no need for public school involvement in drama, art, sports, or music. Since there would be very little if any homework, children could pursue their interests after school. There could be art clubs, music clubs, and sports clubs and so on.

All students would complete a survey immediately following each EBE Experience. The student would use an identifier, not a name when completing the survey. The results of the survey would be used to gauge the experience not the student individually. If only a small number of students answered the survey correctly, it would be assumed that the experience was not designed properly and not that the students were not intelligent enough to understand.

Random classrooms across the USA would be video recorded so the EBE educational designers could evaluate the delivery of the experience. This could lead to improved training of the EBE Facilitators.

It would be assumed EBE designers would be waiting to analyze the results and quickly begin working on refining the experience for the following year. The effectiveness of each experience would be rated by the results of the survey. If the results were not deemed successful, the developer educators could be replaced.

The high school graduation Diploma would be granted when the student participated in all the required experiences.

Note: Participation would be the only requirement for a high school diploma.

Since traditional subject matter would not be taught at the high school level, subject matter teachers could be trained to conduct experience-based education although successful experience-based teachers could come from a diverse pool of ages and occupations. Colleges could offer degrees for EBE facilitators.

With EXPERIENCED BASED EDUCATION:

Facilitator/teachers could be paid on a commission per student graduate basis or a salary plus bonus based on completion percentages.

Facilitator/teachers could be paid the same amount throughout the USA, with adjustments based on the cost of living by region.

EBE facilitators would be taught skills typically associated with successful athletic coaches. Psychological counseling, facilitator, and team building skills would be sauté after, while specific subject matter knowledge would only be necessary at the Elementary or college level. EBE facilitators could work on contractual agreements and could change regions, schools, and school systems at random because the curriculum would be the same everywhere in the USA.

With the EBE system lesson plans would be "hard-wired" into the program. Once trained, significant preparation by facilitators would not be necessary. In many cases, the student teams would be totally on their own to carry out the requirements of the educational experience. EBE Facilitators would just guide the process.

There is little doubt in my mind the school of the not too distant future will not have teachers or facilitators. A group of Students will be given a set of materials. As they examine what they have available, they will create an experience where they will learn information a group of specialists assisted by artificial intelligence predicted would occur. Imagine how interesting and useful this type of education will be.

One of the best resources for curriculum developers and facilitators of EBE would be the Association for Talent Development. (Formerly, the American Society for Training and Development)

All students who completed the requirements for a high school diploma could add their names and preferences to the National College List.

All colleges that received federal or state funding would be required to participate. Colleges would randomly draw their freshmen class from the list of graduates. Colleges would be rated on the successful employment of their graduates.

The goals of High School level EBE could be as follows:

• Learn the difference between right and wrong

• Identify a career path

• Create a life plan

• Learn decision-making theory and the consequences of poor decision-making

• Learn to socialize with and understand people

• Learn to Work in teams

• Learn to respect people of all ages, ethnicity, and status

• Learn basic communication in two foreign languages.

• Learn the value of and how to conduct research

• Learn the fundamentals of business entrepreneurship

• Personal money management

• Understand work for pay concepts

• Learn how to find and apply for a job

• Learn networking and career advancement techniques

• Identify personal strengths and weaknesses and learn methods to take advantage of strengths and overcome personal weaknesses

• Learn the real-world role of reading, writing, math, and science

• Travel to, meet and communicate with people in a foreign country

• Learn good work habits

• Learn job safety such as the Right to Know Law

• Learn to practice good health habits, nutrition, and exercise

One of the required experiences should be to have many opportunities for high school students to connect with businesses in America and foreign countries. Students would learn basic words in two foreign languages and all students would fly to a foreign country. Communication with and travel to foreign countries is routine in business today. This experience would provide a tremendous advantage to American high school graduates.

It is unrealistic to think we can educate aimless children. We need a system that gives them purpose and direction before we funnel them into college or employment.

At the beginning with EBE, there will be a learning period. Adopting EBE will have bumps and potholes along the way. Traditional educators will fight it. Because there will be one-year periods between specific EBE sessions, hard data could be gathered and meaningful adjustments made. Over time as EBE is practiced, new skills and training methods will be adopted to refine the EBE format.

Currently, our schools are dispensing hundreds of thousands if not millions of totally unprepared kids every year. Education methods have not changed for hundreds of years. We need to change the education system and fast. Mistakes are worth the risk. The current system can't go anywhere but up. We owe it to these kids and our nation.

Chapter 4

Manufacturing Jobs

One has to question how unions gained power in the United States. Were conditions that bad in the auto industry? The auto industry was already paying higher wages than most similar jobs. Sure, people worked long hours, but everybody worked long hours in 1936. It appears communists influenced the sit-down strike and other union organizing conflicts. Some strikers admitted they were influenced by Communist-led strikes in Europe.

Did communists put ideas in the minds of vulnerable workers to make them believe the worst of their employers? Employers and managers lives were being threatened, factories were being sabotaged, and they responded in kind. Did employers have a choice?

I am always disappointed in the media who take the side of the Unions and ignore their gangster side. There was always an atmosphere of danger during a strike. I can remember seeing all the windows broken out of factories. We were always hearing stories about manager's homes being vandalized, beatings, slashed tires, death threats. These tactics were common knowledge in Michigan where I was born.

Unions made it impossible to build a quality vehicle. To offset the strong-arm union tactics, car manufacturers made the toughest bully types managers. They were less apt to be pushed around by the tough union shop stewards. This antagonism was directly opposed to what is necessary to build quality products. Where I grew up, you would routinely hear,

> *"I would not buy a Chevy; I see*
> *how they are made."*

Imagine having to deal with aggressive union thugs in your own factory.

In contrast, in Japan where teamwork is widely practiced, and quality is world class, managers tend to be quiet good listener types. This encourages employee cooperation and support for following best practices for quality.

A typical US Auto union tactic is to create hundreds of grievances then trade them to force changes or protect employees who should be penalized. It was common for unions to write up a grievance for all of the jobs in a factory when a new model car came online.

Can you imagine management dealing with hundreds of grievances when they were trying to build a new car?

Can you imagine trying to build a quality car made of thousands of intricate parts while dealing with this kind of resistance every day?

Can you imagine owning a factory and being required to have an office inside your factory manned by people whose job it is to slow production, protect employees who steal, are drunk on the job, or don't show up for work?

Walk into any unionized auto factory and that is what you are likely to find. Union demands can include approval of every single job in a factory. It should not be a surprise when unionized companies relocate to a foreign country or close.

All you have to do is spend a little time in a unionized auto factory to see how little some workers produce for very high pay. In Poland where you will find some of the finest skilled tradesmen in the world, with great pride, you might find them coming in on their own time to paint and service their machinery. Unions have made this type of activity against the law in the United States. The United States government has spent billions protecting unions. Do you know there is a Union rule the does not allow auto manufacturers to teach teamwork? So sad, it is funny.

> *"ORGANIZATIONAL CHANGE AND DEVELOPMENT ... One option available to GM is to reduce the UAW's fear that introducing teams will reduce jobs by increasing productivity"* **Donald D. White, David A. Bednar**

I will admit the early auto-manufacturing corporation owners were not perfect, but they were not fools. Back in the day, factories had doctors and housing developments for workers, they knew workers needed to be satisfied and make enough money to buy the products they were manufacturing.

Look at these leading companies of today.

• Adobe Systems

• Advanced Micro Devices (AMD)

- Agilent Technologies

- Apple Inc.

- Applied Materials

- Cisco Systems

- eBay

- Google

- Hewlett-Packard

- Intel

- Intuit

- Juniper Networks

- LSI Logic

- National Semiconductor

- NetApp

- Nvidia

- Oracle Corporation

No unions here. People who own companies are not fools. Common sense says to create a good working environment. Unions always want to take credit for job changes and benefits that would have happened anyway.

Look at some of the benefits you might find with these non-union companies.

Free video games

- A room for massages and meditation

- Game rooms with pool tables, ping-pong, etc.

- Two a month house cleaning

- Fertility treatments

- Free Food

- Free wash and fold clothes

- Haircuts

- Vacation Cash

- Field Trips to foreign countries

- $500 Baby Cash

- Parental Leave

- Jam Room, Bring your guitar and drums.

"Robert Noyce, co-founder of Intel Corp, remaining non-union is an

essential for survival for most of our companies. If we had the work rules that unionized companies have, we'd all go out of business. This is a very high priority for management here. We have to retain flexibility in operating our companies. The great hope for our nation is to avoid those deep, deep divisions between workers and management which can paralyze action."

Organizing Silicon Valley's High Tech Workers by David Bacon

Laws have been passed that give Unions the upper hand in negotiations. For example, requiring the company to prove every detail while allowing the Union to make preposterous claims that have no basis in fact. Secret negotiations have allowed strikes to continue for weeks until the company agreed to hire the Union boss's kids are some of the allegations rumored to have occurred. Live broadcast of union-management negotiations would probably eliminate this unfair advantage.

"Fiat Chrysler workers in Detroit have filed a class-action suit against the auto manufacturer

and their union, United Auto Workers, requesting refunds of all of their membership dues from 2009 through 2015. They say the manufacturer bribed the union leaders, tainting their collective bargaining agreements.

Internet News

Had the unions not gained a foothold in the USA things would surely be different today. Wages would not be as high for sure. The middle class would be a much larger percentage of the population. There would be good benefits, but they would be much lower in cost because all wages would be lower even for professionals. A burger meal deal might cost $1.99 instead of $7.99, as it does today. The cost of living would surely be lower. The money all American's earn would buy far more than it does today.

It seems that anytime a major economic factor has been distorted; that is changed by artificial means such as union pressure rather than supply and demand, it has a long-term negative economic impact. When unions gained power, they pressured companies to pay higher wages and that seemed fine.

The unions took credit for creating the so-called middle class. That middle class was largely limited to the North East and Midwest in what is now known as the economically depressed rust belt. Large portions of the population in other parts of the county only got the higher prices and missed the middle-class part.

As wages rose so did prices. I remember changing prices on milk cartons at my grocery store job the same day a strike was settled. Over time, this made the cost of living in the USA much higher than the rest of the world. Now China, South Korea, Vietnam, Taiwan, India, Mexico, and soon Africa with lower costs of living whittle away at whatever industry is left in the USA.

A recent distortion that had a huge economic effect was the easy mortgage money policy that led people to speculate in the housing market. In this case, artificially lax mortgage qualification requirements caused housing prices to inflate leading to the recent Great Recession of 2008. Repercussions of this collapse are still being felt today.

About thirty years ago following the many upheavals and purges in China, they began to encourage the Chinese people to create factories and businesses. Since then, the Chinese have built roads, bullet trains, millions of homes, dams, and bridges. They copied American capitalism. Today China has a huge and growing middle class. All without unions.

> *"I think the rise of China is one of the great events of all economic and human history, and I think this will be overwhelmingly a positive thing for the region and the world."*

> **Paul Keating**

If you're wondering why Buicks are selling so well in China, It is thought that Buick's popularity in China stems from photos that show that the father of Chinese democracy, Sun Yatsen; the first premier of China, Zhou Enlai; and the last emperor, Puyi, owned Buicks.

A huge middle class would have grown in the United States even without the Unions. In addition, because the cost of living would not have grown so high, we would still have most of those high paying manufacturing jobs that we have lost to foreign countries.

One of the important issues with car manufacturing is staying ahead of the curve, having new advanced cars ahead of the competition. In recent years, US car companies have a poor record when it comes to leading-edge trend-setting vehicles. To get in the lead requires moving quickly. How do you expect car companies to move quickly when you have to ask the union's permission every time you turn around?

Sadly, unions are clearly against profit. Profit is the money left over after all the bills are paid. Manufacturing companies are fearful of even saying the word profit. Why should profit be a dirty word? Because the union said, they wanted the profit. This is all while Toyota, Honda, Nissan were killing the Big 3 with better quality and high-tech new cars. These companies use their profit for research to make better cars and new products. It is clear to see that the American manufacturers are never going to be able to compete with unions at their heels. Big advances in cars are yet to come and it is going to require huge profits to develop them. Whom would you bet on?

About the time, the collapse of the housing market occurred General Motors was just about 2 years away from turning the profitability corner. Thousands of early-retired GM employees would be old enough to where the company would no longer be required to pay retirement and health insurance for them. GM would be profitable again. The downsizing gamble was paying off.

When the housing bubble collapse occurred in 2008 many financial intuitions and companies were about to go out of business. The obvious economic solution was to pour money into the economy and save the companies that were too important to fail. The Government imposed an unusual bailout plan for General Motors by forcing them to go out of business then buying them out rather than allow GM to declare a Chapter 11 Bankruptcy.

This legally questionable action weakened the company and strengthened the Union by reorganized the Company giving GM a share, the UAW Union a Share, the Canadian government a share, and the Federal Government a Share. GM stock and bondholders lost everything when the Government ignored investor due process. Many believe this action was against the law and set a frightening precedent for the future of stock and bond investments and bankruptcy law.

When GM went out of business all of their previous debt and contractual commitments ended. This is the moment; the USA lost a huge number of its manufacturing jobs. GM dropped to just four car lines, closed huge factories and caused hundreds of car dealerships to close. Chrysler and Ford downsized as well. In cities and towns all over America, building construction stopped while restaurants, barbershops, thousands of businesses large and small collapsed within a few weeks. Lost in the melee were hundreds of small job shops whose skilled workers supported the auto industry. The Obama administration chose to sacrifice these businesses and skilled workers to save the Union.

> *"Michigan's factories employed nearly 900,000 workers in 2000. That total collapsed during the Great Recession (after 2007) when Michigan lost almost half its manufacturing jobs, down to 454,900 at the depth of the recession. Manufacturing jobs rebounded to 607,000 by the end of 2017, but that remains far*

below its peak level." **DETROIT FREE PRESS**

Had the Obama Administration chose to let GM declare a normal bankruptcy and loaned them money to "weather the storm", GM could have renegotiated their Union contracts and weakened the Union's stranglehold on the corporation? Negotiating lower wages could have saved thousands of GM jobs. About 60 thousand GM jobs were lost in Flint Michigan alone. Nationwide millions of jobs were lost. Many of those were high paying middle-class manufacturing jobs. The Midwest would be in much better shape today and GM would be a "powerhouse", rather than a vulnerable also-ran. Those are the jobs, the experts say, we will never see again.

"Otherwise, calling the bailout a success is like applauding the recovery of a drunken driver after an accident while ignoring the condition of the family he severely maimed."

Daniel J. Ikenson   Subcommittee on Regulatory Affairs, Stimulus Oversight, and Government

Spending Committee on Oversight and Government Reform United States House of Representatives

Years ago, federal funds would be made available for a county Economic Development director. Each time a new person would come in all fired up about how he or she was going to bring new business to the area. Early on, they would give talks to all the service clubs and it was clear they did not know the house rules. One time one of these rookie Economic Directors told the union they could not attempt to organize a new company thinking about coming to the area. He was gone in the blink of an eye. I always knew no new business would locate in the area with the first order of business a union organization meeting. I can only imagine how many more businesses we would have in Michigan and throughout the United States if we did not have unions. Think of all the factories and jobs that we would still have. Wow makes me tear up.

Periodically, American unions will give lip service to how they want to help the company improve quality, support teamwork and so on. However, history shows their leaders only know how to attack and cause trouble. They would rather have the company fail and workers lose their jobs than negotiate for realistic wages and benefits. All one has to do is read the growing list of companies that have relocated or gone out of business under union pressure. One can only hope for a complete reversal of Union attitudes for America to be a great manufacturing power again.

Obviously, there is no doubt the aggressive Democrat supported unions are detrimental to industrial growth in the USA. If we want to compete on a global scale, Unions must be less antagonistic and truly supportive of profitable corporations. Actually, I do not see this happening without government pressure and even that is unlikely. So sad, as we could have so many more great jobs and opportunities for growth.

Today America has vocal groups of socialists, communists or Progressives, as some like to call them. Obviously, many US Progressive politicians are clearly anti-business, calling them greedy and "fat cats". We in the US are such fools.

Interesting also is the constant banter to raise the minimum wage. Raising the minimum wage usually does more harm than good as many jobs are lost and it only affects a small portion of the workforce. Strong job demand, on the other hand, raises the wages of all workers. Our only chance to regain economic power is to beat the foreign manufacturers at their own game. Pure unbridled Capitalism built America. Nothing else is going to generate the profits necessary for paying down the debt, rebuilding the middle class, maintain bridges, schools, roads, health care services, and military power Americans expect. How long can we continue to spend trillions of dollars more than we bring in each year? Some believe higher taxes are the solution to all of these problems. That should scare the average American to death.

Part of high school should be to learn about business. With young people knowing how to make money maybe we will not have them hoping for a minimum wage job. Now, we have kids leaving high school thinking there is nothing for them to do. Moreover, that is how they respond they do nothing. By contrast, the Chinese people see nothing but opportunity. It sickens me to think we have politicians who thrive on our kids being passive bottom feeders looking for handouts.

About 15 years ago, I began inventing and designing products for online retail markets as a hobby. Soon I was importing my products from

China. It was easy to do. After a few years, I felt it would be great if I could find a US manufacturer for one of my products.

On two occasions, I sent emails to 15 companies in my area whose websites indicated they were capable of manufacturing what I needed. I invited them to dinner, my treat, to discuss doing business. I didn't have to buy any dinners as I only received two feeble responses. One company said, send them a sample and they would look it over. A second company said if I could not find anybody to make it, call them back. I assumed from this response that these 15 businesses were not really interested in new business and would not likely provide good service if they did get the job.

In contrast, I contacted a Chinese manufacturer. I sent them a crude drawing of a new item I had designed. Less than 24 hours later, they sent me a picture of the item.   Not a drawing, they had actually made the plastic part. American companies are going to have to learn to hustle and scrounge for business if they expect to be competitive on the world stage. Our world competitors know our weaknesses and take advantage of them every day.

If we want to get manufacturing jobs back, we must lower our design and tooling costs. Start with one design and tooling center such as Kettering University in Michigan. Anyone who has a product they want to make can get free designing and tooling of the product. As long as the product is manufactured in the USA. (Tooling is a manufacturing term that means the molds required to make a product.) Manufacturers around the USA could bid on manufacturing the products. Additional design centers could be added as needed. If American manufacturers really want to get back in the game, they need to be willing to accept small orders. Many times, eventually those small orders become large orders. Hundreds of products sold by Walmart, Target, Sears, Amazon, and eBay could easily be manufactured in the USA.

American manufacturer's tooling costs are not competitive. Designing and tooling costs run 300% to 500% more in the USA compared to China. Chinese companies are willing to take the risk to make money on sales rather on the design and tooling. Design and tooling in the USA can take many months and sometimes years. Design and tooling in China require a much shorter time period which means products get to market quicker. Other than unions, I believe design, tooling costs and time to production are the biggest deterrents to new manufacturing in the USA.

Access to American manufacturers is much more difficult compared to their foreign counterparts. US manufacturers need a free US version of the business-to-business website, Alibaba. The Alibaba website is not well designed. I am sure something could be much better exclusively for USA manufacturers.

I suggest, offering a US government-shipping subsidy for products manufactured in the US shipped to retail customers in foreign countries. The cost would be nominal and a great incentive, especially for small US companies, just starting out Most, cargo ships departing the USA are half-empty. I am sure some great shipping rates could be negotiated.

Chapter 5

Election Process

"In 2004, the federal debt was $7.3 trillion. This rose to $10 trillion when the housing bubble burst four years later. Today, it exceeds $18 trillion and is projected to approach $21 trillion by 2019. When you break this down to an amount per taxpayer, the numbers are substantial. It has more than doubled over the past 11 years, rising from $72,051 per taxpayer in 2004 to $154,161 today. As the debt continues higher, the liability of every taxpayer is also rising. The change in the amount of the federal debt per taxpayer from 2004 to 2015 represents an average annual increase of 7.16%. This is much more than the average annual wage increase during the same period."

Forbes

A rule of thumb for individual personal debt is about 3 times earnings. So, if you made say, $60,000 a year your total debt limit should be about $180,000. The current annual United States income in taxes citizens pay is $3.5 trillion. If we apply the same three times earnings family debt, our maximum debt would be about $10.5 trillion. The actual National debt to which we are adding over 1 trillion per year is $18 trillion or $8 trillion over what our imaginary family could afford. The equivalent of purchasing 160,000 Boeing 737's, 40 million Lamborghini's, 267 million Chevy Volts, or 2.5 trillion happy meals.

1,000,000,000,000 = one trillion

Some politicians say we should not worry about our debt as long as we can make the payments. They say as long as the payments are a small percentage of the GDP it will not be a problem. Sounds like my credit card company. I think employed people in the United States should be worried about our out of control national debt.

Financial institutions in the USA are the result of government intervention. Politicians cannot blame Wall Street as they have created the structure that

Wall Street employs. The way to remove big monies influence is to create a fixed grant to politicians running for national office. President $200 million Senators $100 million Representatives $40 million, or something. Anyone could contribute toward the pool. The additional money would be divided equally between the candidates regardless of party affiliation. Any money the candidates did not spend would be put back into the pool.

Any elected government official should not be able to profit as a direct result of having been elected. While in office, all investments by the elected official, family and business associates would be announced 60 days prior to the transaction. Good deals on investments should be made available to all.

An independent accounting of assets would be required before and after the term of office. In addition, exorbitant amounts paid in excess of costs for speaking engagements and appearances during or following the holding of office would be considered bribery and prosecuted as such. As would excessive consulting fees, free vacations, Vicuna Coats, etc. One must ask, how the Clintons amassed 50 million dollars in just 3 years following the election. I guess they give really good speeches and offer snacks and drinks afterward. Shouldn't America be above all that?

All meetings with lobbyists should be videotaped and made available to the public.

In my estimation, all politicians play to the crowd. That is, they must sacrifice something they believe in to gain election or save legislation. That is nothing new; it was probably true in Roman days. What I would like to be confident about, is that the politician is not sacrificing beliefs for reelection money but rather for the good of the Nation.

We must change our election process so elected officials will not benefit from the bribery like contributions of interest groups that is rampant today. Every problem we have in the country is HUGE! $18 trillion National debt, 3 million criminals in jail, 46 million people on food stamps, 20 million undocumented immigrants, $3 trillion in health care, and 600,000 high school dropouts, all these things were a lot more solvable before they grew to these gigantic proportions. We need lawmakers that are beholden to no one.

Before TV and the internet, it made sense to spread the Presidential election process over a long period. Our current method of securing candidates for national office is out of date, ridiculously expensive and encourages corruption. It bothers many Americans that elections seem to go to the wealthiest of our citizens. Whether true or not, it surely appears politicians are controlled by something other than what is best for America.

Suggested Election process:

• The campaign period should be about 180 days.

• It would begin with a televised introduction of the candidates wishing to run for office, President and so on.

• The candidates would receive a Federal grant and spend up to $X Million during the next 60 days during which the candidates would compete with other candidates of the same party.

• Following the 60 days, 1 week of Caucasus would be held. Followed by the party conventions.

• A fixed sum of money would be Government granted to the chosen Presidential, Congressional and House candidates to be used during a 60-day period prior to the election.

- The candidates could not receive additional private funds or exceed the granted funds spending limit.

Chapter 6

Health Care

It seems appropriate that quality medical care at an affordable cost should be available to all US citizens. Because within reason we can afford it. The question to me is how to provide healthcare that is cost effective and the best quality that Americans have come to expect.

The problem is that with Medicaid, Medicare and Obama Care there appears to be no cost control, no incentives to reduce cost and rampant waste. Currently, the shocking annual cost of health care in the USA is about 3.2 trillion dollars or about $9,000 per citizen. This cost is about 85% per person higher than other countries that provide health care such as Canada, Australia, England, and France. As expected, 32% goes to hospital care and 20% goes to physicians and clinics. It is obvious these two major cost factors need to be reduced if we are going to provide free healthcare to the poor.

"Medicaid is now the largest health insurance program in the United State, covering about 74

million Americans with low
incomes and disabilities, along
with participants in the Children's
Health Insurance Program.
Medicaid is costing our federal
and state governments enormous
amounts of money and the costs
are growing – rising from $553
***billion** in the 2016 federal fiscal*
*year to $565 **billion** in 2017.*
That's about $1 out of every $6
spent on health care in the U.S."

DR. MARC SIEGEL | FOX NEWS

These gigantic government programs are "easy pickens" for dishonest health care providers and organized crime. The poor qualify for Medicaid and it is one of the reasons welfare rolls are not coming down. Reducing poverty automatically improves health care and reduces medical costs. A win, win situation. Reducing medical costs is something we cannot afford not to do.

It appears anywhere we can reduce direct doctor contact and hospital admissions it will have a significant effect on lowering costs. Currently, hospitals are using primarily hospital-owned outpatient care facilities such as doctors' offices and emergency clinics as feeders for the hospital system. This process assures the high cost of medical care will continue is the USA.

It is clear doctors in the USA are paid far more than any other county in the world. Like it or not, high tech equipment, technicians and physicians' assistants will have to take the place of doctors to make a diagnosis and prescribe treatment, if we want to lower costs.

Drug costs are very high. Currently, drug companies patent drugs and they charge as much as they can during to patent period. Then another many times less capable company makes a generic copy and charges much less for the drug. I would like to see drug patents extended indefinitely. The developer of the drug could charge less for the drug initially as they could spread development costs over a longer period. Just to be sure, extending the patent would require a substantial reduction in cost. A formula could be developed for each patent extension requiring a further reduction in cost.

Obesity is a significant factor that adds to the cost of health care. As an abundance of food is available to citizens at all income levels. Abuse of food in the USA is rampant. Some say, epidemic levels. It is a difficult issue. Obesity is a more serious problem among the poor because it negatively affects employability in addition to health.

Currently, food labeling is a joke. Only the well-educated can understand the difference between good and bad fat, cholesterol, etc. Suggested serving sizes are beyond hilarious. Also, a large percentage of the population cannot read.

All food should have a large label. Labels would be red, blue or green. Foods would be divided into 3 categories based on a combination of calories to weight and food value. The total number of calories in the food container would be printed in the center of the label. The label would be positioned on the front and back of the package.

Portion size or calories per portion would not be on the package.

To show fat levels, the label would say something like "Fat High Good", meaning a high amount of fat but not harmful. "Fat High Bad", meaning a high amount of fat but harmful. Salt content should also be shown as a HIGH, MED, and LOW below the calorie number.

People would be advised to develop weight loss and nutrition plans based on label colors:

• Red-labeled food recommended to be eaten in small quantities rarely

• Blue-labeled foods recommended being eaten in moderate amounts.

• Green-labeled foods recommended being eaten as desired

• High sugar content juices, sodas, ice cream would have red labels

• Potato chips, pasta, crackers, bread, and pastries would have red labels

• Most fruit and vegetables would have green labels

• Blue labels would be higher protein lower carbohydrate foods like meat, cheese, and nuts

LOAF OF WHITE BREAD

2,600

FAT-MED-OK
SALT-MED

RED

JAPANESE NOODLES 3.9OZ

260

FAT-HIGH-OK
SALT-HIGH

16OZ LIGHTLY SALTED PEANUTS

2,700

FAT-HIGH-OK
SALT-MED

BLU

8OZ CTN 2% COTTAGE CHEESE

270

FAT-MED-BAD
SALT-HIGH

5OZ ALBACORE TUNA IN WATER

100

FAT-LOW-OK
SALT-LOW

GRN

303 CAN GREEN BEANS

70

FAT-LOW-OK
SALT-MED

Health care is very equipment intensive. We should standardize equipment where possible and use robots and the internet to diagnose, treat patients and maintain equipment. We should encourage competition and have a national Medical Academy Awards ceremony honoring cost reducing advancements in medicine, red carpet and all.

I have great respect for those in the medical professions. However, when looking at the big picture we need a method to lower the cost and offer the highest quality care. It will not be easy. I am confident that technology will eventually make all medical care better and lower in cost.

Today's hospital patient is monitored by high tech machines and many procedures are made faster and simpler than in the past. Soon diagnosing and treating diseases with the application of sensors combined with artificial intelligence will be commonplace. I am concerned that hospitals will fight lowering their costs even though actual hospital costs of health care will fall. Myriad certifications, and accreditations, which require personnel to have advanced degree ratings and titles, are constantly pushing up the cost of hospital care, also.

In the past, we could train someone in one year to become an LPN (Licensed Practical Nurse). Then they came along with an Associate Degree nursing RN Registered Nurse degree. Not to be outdone, colleges started offering bachelor's degree RN nursing programs. You guessed it, now they are pushing for a master's degree APN degree as the standard. In addition, some hospital accreditations are now requiring Ph.D. degree nurses. They are called DNP's. All these nurses expect to be paid much more because of their advanced degrees. All the while the future of healthcare will require less training and improved health care. Personnel needs in the healthcare industry will fall dramatically in the coming years.

Hospitals are in a no-win situation because they all want to be highly rated and ratings are dependent on how many accreditations and certificates they can list. All of these nursing qualifications have the net effect of creating a nursing shortage, which keeps wages high and under control of the accrediting bodies.

The argument the accrediting groups suggest is nurses need all this extra training because people that go to the hospital are sicker. I guess, in the past people felt pretty- well when they went to the hospital.

We ought to be concerned how pressure from accrediting bodies is affecting hospital costs. I wonder to whom and how much accrediting bodies pay to lobby for their cause. Other than raise costs, do these accreditation's do anything more than provide bragging rights?

Seems to me some of this could all be solved by changing the hospital rating system. You know something uniform we could all understand such as, how successful they are with delivering health care. Maybe a 10-point scale or something like that. Makes sense, if hospitals have good outcomes with the patients that would be what people would want to know. I will bet someone could run a dandy hospital with just RN's and LPN's.

I propose a "moon shot" effort to develop a Kiosk style standardized medical care facility. The goal would be to lower the cost of healthcare to where about 70% could be covered out of pocket by the average person. All the best resources could be brought together to create the kiosk system. Microsoft, IBM, Intel, GE, Mayo Clinic, Universities could be involved. It would be mass-produced, easily maintained and updated regularly.

Limited Kiosk Care is already in use. It makes the most sense for the future as many medical advancements are being developed that will not require the huge facilities and expenditures that we experience today. Giant hospitals and highly educated medical personnel will not be necessary in the not too distant future. A byproduct of new technology is that it makes everything easier to do. It will not be long before your cell phone will diagnose most illnesses, provide your complete health status and be of critical importance in your medical care.

Doctors have a new tool to help diagnosis the flu.

Tarajean Lee has recovered after recently testing positive for the flu.

"I was out of work for, for days," Lee said. "It just really knocked me down."

Fortunately, for her, the clinic has a diagnostic tool, a machine that looks for the flu virus in a different way and is far more effective than conventional tests, Dr. Anthony Powell said.

"This test uses what's called nucleic amplification," he said. "It's very accurate, so for Influenza B, it's 100-percent sensitive, and for influenza A, it's 90-95 percent sensitive, so it's much, much better."

"So, we can get you treated when you need the therapy, and we can feel confident that you actually have the flu and that our test is accurate, and we can be proactive in treated members of your family and that can make a big difference in the spread of the flu," Powell said.

MENLO PARK, CA (KRON/CNN)

The Kiosk System should be able to conduct most medical tests, provide prenatal care, perform minor surgery and treatments such as kidney dialysis, X-rays, and follow up on some treatments and therapy following injury and surgery.

"Scientists unveil laser that can monitor your breathing and heartbeat through clothes from three feet away"

"ContinUse Biometrics' nanotechnology can monitor senses without touching

It can measure respiration, lung activity, temperature, blood pressure, pulse wave velocity, glucose, alcohol level and muscle activity through clothing

Particularly useful for people with cardiovascular diseases or diabetes"

DAILY MAIL

Colleges could develop programs such as Medical Kiosk Technician to operate and administer the Kiosk system. Medical records could be automatically maintained, and a video record would be saved that could be referenced by the doctor or patient.

Fees to use the Kiosk would be based on income level and services rendered. It is assumed the fees would be much lower than traditional health care would charge. High volume use of Kiosk Care would likely bring the cost down.

Kiosks could be housed in drug stores, retail outlets, factories, office buildings, housing developments, and any other reasonably accessible location. Companies could buy or lease Kiosks and offer the service to employees. Insurance could be purchased that covered all or part of an individual's health care costs such as hospitalization only.

"CCMB working to make personalized medicine a reality

Scientists can now convert ordinary cells extracted from a patient's body into what are called pluripotent stem cells and use these to develop a variety of organoids – multiple miniaturized and simplified versions of body organs.

*These can then be used to screen
a variety of drugs for the ailment
a person is suffering from and
identify those that are best suited
for him or her."*

Obama Care formalized the process of poverty level citizens receiving free health care. Federal money along with limited State funding covers most of the cost. Therefore, if we think as a nation free health care should be provided free for all. Then we should agree to pay for that added benefit.

Funding health care is not as simple in the USA. We have a large medical insurance lobby; the highest health care costs and we have a large poverty level population. In addition, countries that have free healthcare have a much higher tax rate. The key is to reduce the annual $3.2 TRILLION-dollar cost.

• We could initiate a payroll deduction percentage toward health care.
• All visitors to the USA could pay $100 emergency medical assistance tax per visit. Estimated revenue $600 million. This fee would only make emergency

care available to the visitor not the cost of any exams/procedures, etc.

Charges for medical procedures are confusing at best. Insurers pay a small percentage of the posted price and the patient has no idea how the costs are computed or if they are correct. Billing for hospital care should include doctors' fees. And should be delivered to the patient within 15 days of discharge. Making inquiries and changes with the insurer or hospital is a nightmare. Published charges should be the normal amount actually paid and a standardized fee formula should be created so charges can be understood by the general population. Currently, there is no reasonable way to compare prices or the quality of the medical service offered. I'm sure published fees would stir up a little competition. We could call it, Truth in Medicine.

To lower doctor's fees, negotiate new fee schedules for doctors. Maybe, reduce doctor fees 2% a year for 10 years. For every $1 a doctor discounted from fees, they would normally bill Medicaid or Medicare; they could receive a $0.10 tax credit, or something. For example, if a standard Medicaid payment to the doctor for an appendectomy was $4,000. The doctors who chose not to charge for the procedure would receive a $400 tax credit. Similar tax credit schemes could be developed for drug and medical equipment manufacturers.

Combining the added revenue with cost reductions such as Kiosk Care and lower doctor fees would make the cost much more affordable for all.

Chapter 7

Taxes

The American income tax system is a conundrum. Special interest groups have decimated it to the point that the average citizen does not believe the system is fair. In addition, it is far too complicated. A national sales tax combined with a simpler flat income tax would be welcomed by most Americans. Especially, if the income tax was the same for all without special rates for this or that group or industry. Let groups that need relief plead their case and get direct aid if necessary. That way, the reason for aid and the amount allocated will be clear and above- board, not buried in tax mumbo-jumbo. The entire Tax Code should fit on two pages size 16 font.

Great care should be taken if we were to adopt this type of plan. I would advise for the sales tax to start with .5% and adding .5% every other year for 10 or 12 years. That way it would not be such a shock to our consumer dependent economic system.

Chapter 8

Foreign Relations

Each year countries collectively spend trillions of dollars to defend themselves from their real and perceived enemies. My question is why do we need enemies? Clearly, there are countries and fanatical groups that are threats. Even those enemies should know we would like to be friendly if given the opportunity.

Every day the news services post stories about Russia and China as though they hope the US will go to war any minute. The stories do their best to make people in these countries appear evil and ignorant. To the contrary, we should be doing everything we can to assure the stability of these countries. Major instability in either country could easily start an atomic war that no one would survive.

I am very baffled why we treat Russia and China as enemies. I cannot imagine either country controlling the United States even if we let them walk in and take over. They both have a heck of a time keeping their own citizens happy and economies afloat most of the time, as does the

United States. The added burden of controlling the USA would pull them both under.

The histories of both countries should not negatively reflect on the character, morals, and ethics of today's citizens of these countries. As we say, "they put their pants on one leg at a time." You would find they are proud of their history, families, and traditions. They are also hard workers and especially enjoy a good time. Sound familiar? Why would we want them as enemies?

We in the United States would have equal trouble managing China or Russia. If we attacked China and even if they did not fight back it would be impossible to make enough bullets to kill them all. The Russians are very tough people attacking Russia would probably destroy America in the process even if we won the war.

We as a nation could be a lot friendlier to both nations. We could help them grow food, learn to gamble on sports, learn to play football not soccer, improve their medical care. Surely, we would like them to buy our products. Economic balance is important there is no doubt that improved relations would make it easier when negotiating trade agreements.

I would begin by declaring 2 holidays China Friendship day and Russian Friendship Day. Have programs from both countries on TV. Have parades, the whole shebang. Praise their people; honor their war heroes' astronauts all that stuff. Why not have the crew of a Chinese Aircraft carrier in Times Square on New Year's Eve. This could start to change the atmosphere in the whole world. Expressing genuine friendship without expecting anything in return would change things for the better in all the worlds' relationships. We should attempt to have every Russian and Chinese politician visit the United States, on our nickel, if necessary.

At one time, a friend of mine had two cats. One was older and BIG the other was young and small. The little young cat always wanted to play. The older big cat would tolerate all the activity for a while then the BIG cat would just lay on top of the little cat and that would be the end of playtime.

 Seems to me that a group the USA, Russia, and China together could lay on top of Israel and the Palestinians warring factions and put an end to it. The Palestinians need some major compensation and the Israelis need to give up a something so the Arab nations can save face. In addition, maybe build a joint Russian, Chinese and American military base in the Golan Heights to keep order.

Many refer to countries in the EU and think the United States should become more Socialist. They are small countries with cohesive populations. Socialism may be fine for them. I do not think people realize that if it was not for the United States these countries would not exist.

> *"A recession in Europe could lead to the collapse of the Eurozone, as the single currency would buckle under the political turmoil unleashed by a fresh downturn, a leading investment bank has warned. In a research note titled "Close to the edge", economists at* **Swiss bank Credit Suisse** *warned the fate of monetary union hangs in the balance if Europe's policymakers are unable to ward off another global slump and quell anti-euro populism.*

Not because we won WW2. The reason is the United States is the economic backbone that holds these countries together. Were it not for the economic strength of the USA the world would be much different today. England, France, Greece, Germany, Spain and many other countries do not maintain large armies or have the strength to fight off severe economic stress.

Who buys their cars? Where do their tourists come from? Without the USA, the EU would fall like a house of cards. The USA is economically strong because of capitalism. There should be no shame in having money and power, which is what freedom, allows us to earn. The shame should be not to take advantage of what freedom has to offer and use it

The United States does have an unregistered alien problem. No one is sure how many unregistered aliens there are in the country. Shocking estimates range from 10 to 20 million. It seems to me that we should know who is coming and going in our country. Obviously, for security from terrorism, drug trafficking, and crime, but there are other reasons as well, tracking disease, budgeting services and more.

 Our border with Mexico is the biggest problem. It is estimated that 60% (6 million +) of unregistered aliens are Mexican. The border is big, it is open, and it is estimated one to 2 million people enter the country illegally every year. It is a growing threat that must be addressed. Then they take advantage of our welfare and medical system. To top it off we pay to maintain a court system to handle the over one hundred thousand asylum claims every year.

Below is my idea for a boundary wall that is easy to fabricate inexpensive and difficult to climb.

MEXICO
BOUNDARY WALL

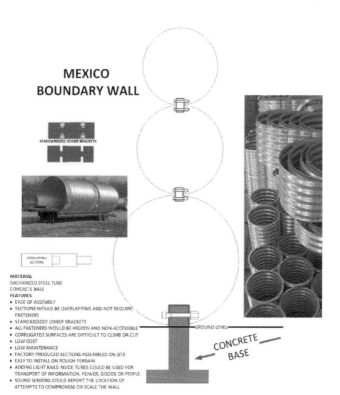

STANDARDIZED JOINER BRACKETS

OVERLAPPING
SECTIONS

MATERIAL
GALVANIZED STEEL TUBE
CONCRETE BASE
FEATURES
- EASE OF ASSEMBLY
- SECTIONS WOULD BE OVERLAPPING AND NOT REQUIRE FASTENERS
- STANDARDIZED JOINER BRACKETS
- ALL FASTENERS WOULD BE HIDDEN AND NON-ACCESSIBLE
- CORRUGATED SURFACES ARE DIFFICULT TO CLIMB OR CUT
- LOW COST
- LOW MAINTENANCE
- FACTORY PRODUCED SECTIONS ASSEMBLED ON SITE
- EASY TO INSTALL ON ROUGH TERRAIN
- ADDING LIGHT RAILS INSIDE TUBES COULD BE USED FOR TRANSPORT OF INFORMATION, POWER, GOODS OR PEOPLE
- SOUND SENSORS COULD REPORT THE LOCATION OF ATTEMPTS TO COMPROMISE OR SCALE THE WALL

GROUND LEVEL

CONCRETE BASE

We should adopt some tougher policies regarding all visitors. I like Australia's policy of requiring everyone entering the country to have a paid ticket to leave. If you are not on that outbound plane, they are going to come and get you.

I think we should sell Mexico on becoming part of the United States. Obviously, many Mexicans must like the United States since they seem to all want to come here. Mexico is already divided into states. They could become territories then part of United States in some manageable sequence. The combination of tourism and industry would make a stable collection of US states in what is now Mexico an economic powerhouse. Love to have Canada also if they wanted to join. Imagine the collective economic value and strength the combined nations would have.

China is both large and geographically isolated. They would not easily function as part of the United States, I don't think. China is on its way to becoming better at being American than America. That is, they are practicing the same rampant Capitalism that America did in its past. You get the feeling the first thing they teach kids in China is Salesmanship.

I do not think we should be concerned about their military aggression. I would like China to ignore Taiwan, although it is a thorn in their side. I think we could come to some conciliatory arrangement that lets them save face and move on. The old guard communists in China are being replaced by younger people who see the value of good business relationships rather than making enemies.

In China, there is a growing fear that younger educated men well indoctrinated in the good life would not make tough soldiers. I would not want to test that theory, but I do think the Chinese are not as aggressively postured as our press's depiction.

I think we have an excellent opportunity to establish friendship as our primary relationship with China before they build a giant high-tech military complex, which needs to be maintained and prove its value.

Radical Islam is a serious world issue. We must maintain an aggressive stance as radical Islam would make Hitler's Germany look like a vacation resort. I believe the only long-term solution is educating their young about freedom, science, sex, wealth, video games and the internet. When they grow up, they will ignore the radical religious dictators. A few million-tablet computers and a good internet connection would do more to weaken the religious fanatics than bombs.

I am baffled by women in the USA that seem oblivious to the consequences of radical Islam. I guess they think it is OK to be stoned to death for wearing a skirt

Chapter 9

Environmeddle

Wouldn't it be wonderful if we could significantly reduce poverty, crime, grow the middle class, develop new clean energy, and improve the environment? We can, and it is relatively easy.

Of course, we should be concerned about Global Changes and actively support reasonable experiments to offset negative effects.

Of course, we should support all reasonable opportunities to raise the standard of living.

Of course, we should support all reasonable opportunities to improve the environment.

Special interest groups that likely benefit financially from "stirring the pot" on these issues are trying to hold the country hostage by making it appear that their solutions are the only viable answers. Their goal is to make people feel guilty for causing them. On the other hand, they act innocent as if they just arrived on the scene. They pounce on one study after another. Each time claiming disaster is just around the corner. They use these issues to cloud over other horrendous problems like poverty, the failing education system, drug use, crime, and world conflict.

They believe higher taxes are the solution for these imprecise ongoing issues. All the while growing their fiefdoms built on tax dollars and contributions from gullible philanthropists. They do everything they can to divert attention from many other important issues such as poverty and crime. The sad reality is, their proposed spending cannot really solve these issues and may only make them worse. While at the same time, the important issues for everyday citizens are ignored.

Global warming is not going to be solved by exchanging promises with other countries. The only chance we have to make a modest effect on global warming is from a position of economic abundance. Use the money to fund the development of technology that reduces warming. If global warming is truly a problem, a strong move to Capitalism is our only chance for survival.

Many regions are likely to benefit from Global Warming. History will show natural disasters in the USA benefit the affected region's economy. The money spent to counter rising oceans and so on will boost the economy in those regions. The northern climes will have longer growing seasons and more visitors spending vacation money. Think about it. Where would Venice be without its canals? Holland without its dikes. Even the ancient Greeks dug canals and created harbors. Diverting resources ahead of the problem is just another tax burden we do not need. With all the other problems we have, aging infrastructure and so on, to spend trillions on preventing global warming should be considered a crime.

The obvious solution to global warming is atomic energy. Nothing is cleaner or safer.

> *"Remember too that nuclear power plants are the single greatest contributor to reducing emissions of carbon and other greenhouse gases into the atmosphere. It is nuclear energy that provides over 70% of America's zero-emission energy. This is why so many environmentalists concerned with climate change are now loudly proclaiming that more nuclear energy is a necessary component*

of man's corrective actions going forward."

Jerry Paul, nuclear engineer, attorney and former member of the Florida Legislature

So far, the evidence is contrary to my belief that wind power is having some unknown negative effect on climate. I wish I were more comfortable with it. Not to mention they are partially funded with billions in tax dollars wind generators are seriously ugly. I believe that 80,000 wind generators in the US and the added hundreds of thousands worldwide are having yet an undiscovered negative impact.

Yes, I know, it's just wind. I suspect wind patterns have not changed in millions of years. Do we know what problems a change in wind patterns could cause? Soon we will have 800,000 of these wind machines churning around the world. Do we really know what effect they will have?

I think banks of turbines in more wind prone western areas could create a sort of buffer that causes airflow to change from past patterns. Increasing polar vortex and nor'easter activity could be a result. Warming the north by drawing cold air from the pole into the Midwest and northeast states. Melting the northern ice cap while building the southern. It just seems that 800,000 giant wind turbines have to affect something. Hope, it's not catastrophic.

One proven effect of wind generators is raising temperatures at ground level. I believe warmer surface temperatures combined with reduced air circulation could potentially speed vegetation decay, which produces methane. Methane is even worse than carbon dioxide in the atmosphere. Right now, these giant windmills seem harmless enough. I hope wind generators are not causing some irreversible environmental damage or climate phenomena such as tornado clusters and polar vortex storms.

We know burning carbon-based fuels releases carbon dioxide. Carbon dioxide in the atmosphere acts a barrier, prevents heat from escaping, and could over time cause temperatures worldwide to slowly warm. In addition, we know trees absorb carbon dioxide and store it in wood fiber. I am baffled as to why a worldwide campaign is not underway to plant trees on every spare piece of soil we can find. I would, and I expect millions of others would contribute to such a cause.

Chapter 10

Nothing to it

If a few people were sitting chatting on a park bench in Lisbon Portugal in the year 1491, their discussion would be limited by the belief that the Sun went around the earth. Many of that era still believed the world was flat. Christopher Columbus and others soon proved to the contrary. Widely accepted also was that the earth was created in 7 days. Many of that period would be absolutely certain of these fundamental beliefs.

Moving forward 450 years or so, new evidence suggested that the earth and everything else was created as the result of a big bang. An incomprehensibly hot and small particle exploded and created the world we live in as it expands today. There is considerable evidence to prove that this is what happened.

Now scientists are moving forward trying to figure out what, if anything, existed before the big bang.

Well, as a final comment, I would like to add my name as someone who denies what most people believe is fact today. That is, that our existence was created from NOTHING. I believe science will prove that there has always been SOMETHING. Every other explanation attempting to prove that some entity or phenomenon started it all from NOTHING is totally illogical.

Yes, but you are going to argue, how did SOMETHING get here? My answer, it was always here, it has no creator or creation point. But since the universe is SOMETHING, it just makes more sense that if we are made of SOMETHING that we came from SOMETHING. In other words, Theory #1 is NOTHING = SOMETHING. VS Theory #2 SOMETHING = SOMETHING. If there was always SOMETHING, it fits, makes sense. Because there is no way to make something from nothing. Remember NOTHING is NOTHING, not a fleck of dust, a grain of sand, no air, no molecules, elements or cells, NOTHING. Think of it this way, you are in the kitchen and you are going to make a meal, but your kitchen is just empty space... Where would you begin? Exactly!

51066146R00086

Made in the USA
Columbia, SC
13 February 2019